A Girlfriend's Guide to Personal Finance

*Friendly Advice for Managing Your Money
with Confidence*

Hannah Boundy, CFA

Cedarstone Advisors
Westlake Village, CA

First Edition, 2018
Copyright© 2018 Cedarstone Advisors

Published by:
Cedarstone Advisors
2945 Townsgate Road, Suite 200
Westlake Village, CA 91361
(888) 571-5582

978-0-9996143-0-3 (Print)
978-0-9996143-1-0 (E-Readers)

The information contained in this book is provided for general purposes and should not be construed as investment advice. Cedarstone Advisors makes no representations or warranties about the accuracy or completeness of the information contained in this book. Any citations provided are offered as a matter of convenience and are not intended to imply that Cedarstone Advisors endorses, sponsors, promotes and/or is affiliated with the owners of or participants in those sources, or endorses any information contained in those sources, unless expressly stated otherwise. The content of this book does not necessarily represent the actual views or opinions of Cedarstone Advisors or any of its employees. Information in this book should be used at your own risk. Past performance does not guarantee future results. Securities investments involve risk; returns in such investments vary and may involve gain or loss. The materials and content herein are not a substitute for obtaining professional tax, personal financial planning, or other relevant financial advice from a qualified person or firm.

Book and Cover Design: Kelly Cleary, www.kellyclearygraphics.com
Editor: Tammy Ditmore, www.editmore.com
Project Manager: Marla Markman, www.MarlaMarkman.com
Cover Photo: Cecily Breeding, www.cecilybreeding.com

Printed in the United States of America
24 23 22 21 20 19 18   10 9 8 7 6 5 4 3 2 1

For Julie, Jeanne, and KK.
You are my favorites.

For all of the women who choose to be heroines.

And for Ruth who hated chocolate but loved people.

Contents

Chapter 4

Chapter 5

Chapter 7
I Hate Exercise (but Still Run)!

Chapter 8
Every Girl Needs at Least Two Purses:

Chapter 9
Motherhood and Raising Financially

Chapter 19
How to Prepare for the Unexpected 199

PART 6: Being Enough 203

Chapter 20
Confidence and Contentment 205

Appendix A
The "Keeping Track of Everything" Worksheet 211

Appendix B
Judging Quality 213

Introduction

Above all, be the heroine of your life, not the victim.

—NORA EPHRON,
1996 WELLESLEY COMMENCEMENT ADDRESS

NOT LONG AFTER ENTERING the field of financial planning, I became acutely aware of how often women
get the short end of the stick when it comes to finances.
I came to this conclusion while observing client-advisor
interactions during business meetings. I noticed that these
meetings were often dominated by men—even when the
client was a woman. I don't think this is intentional or
necessarily a bad thing, especially in my office because I
work with the best men; they are wonderful, and I love
them. Nevertheless, women's unique concerns too often get
overlooked in male-dominated meetings, which are bound
to happen in my field because finance is a profession dominated by men.

In the U.S. only 20 percent of financial advisors and 16
percent of CFA® charterholders are women.[1] Most of my
clients are baby boomers, and most are couples with one
spouse—typically the man—earning a living for the family.
Although our culture has certainly shifted in recent years to
become more accepting of women working and men staying home, in my professional experience, that arrangement
remains less common.

In my client-meeting-observation role, I have also noticed
that it's typical for one spouse to function as the "money"
spouse and the other spouse to be in the dark about the
household finances. This pattern of handling household

finances leads to two unfortunate consequences: (1) the in-the-dark spouse feels uncomfortable asking questions and being involved during meetings with financial professionals; and (2) if something happens to the "money" spouse, the survivor has no clue what to do about their finances. In my experience, the in-the-dark spouse is usually the woman. Some women have simply allowed their husbands to handle this role for the sake of convenience, while others have relinquished any hands-on role because they find financial topics intimidating—an attitude that may leave them particularly vulnerable to unethical financial advisors in emergencies.

I am a huge believer in empowerment—especially when it comes to women—and I believe education is the key to empowering all individuals to make smart decisions. My primary goal in writing this book is to provide information that improves or enriches readers' lives. My secondary goal is to provide financial information that will benefit female readers in particular; this book focuses on situations that women are more likely to face and delivers information in a style that is more female-friendly. Ladies, consider this book your chance to get your questions answered without having to ask them at an intimidating meeting full of intimidating men in intimidating suits.

I love to learn new things, and I hope that you do too. My hope is that this book will provide you with a basic understanding of how to manage your money and plan for your future whether you're married, divorced, widowed, engaged, single, or otherwise. I want to help you understand professional jargon and complex concepts so that you can recognize when someone is trying to take advantage of you. In any venture, you need to be fully informed if you want to make smart decisions. After reading this book, you should be able to sit down with your financial advisor, banker, lender, or bill collector and feel confident asking questions and demanding answers that make sense.

This is not your average "personal finance" book. If it was, I probably wouldn't want to read it—let alone write it. I've acquired a variety of personal finance books from numerous sources, but I find most of them to be cheesy and insincere—especially the ones with titles like *How to Become a Billionaire Tomorrow* that read like a tacky infomercial.

In my opinion, there are two main types of personal finance books. The first is the get-rich-quick guide with a "foolproof" scheme that turns you into a millionaire overnight. I have not written that kind of book. I think such "schemes" are often dangerous, sometimes illegal, and lead to bankruptcy far more often than they produce wealth. I don't believe in get-rich-quick schemes, and I would never try to sell you one. The other type of common personal finance book gives you step-by-step instructions for reducing debt and increasing savings. I have not written that kind of book either. For some people, throwing out credit cards and starting over with a realistic budget can be important steps on their financial journey, and I won't criticize that approach. I know a lot of people who have found such methods very helpful and often, getting your debt under control is an important first step on the road toward financial security. However, I think too many people stop there because they don't know what to do next.

This book is about what comes next. Once you've figured out how to survive, financially speaking, your next goal is learning to thrive, and I want to help you do just that.

This book is about smart simplicity. I want you to know the basics of personal finance so that you can make informed decisions and be at peace with the state of your wealth. I'm not here to teach you about derivatives or REITS. This book won't make you a master of finance. But it will hopefully give you a firm foundation for meeting your financial goals *and* help you avoid phony investment schemes and unwise money management approaches.

This book is organized in a loosely chronological order based on life stages that most women experience, but the topics are largely universal and applicable to a variety of situations. We will start off by considering why all this money talk matters in Part 1. Then, in Part 2, I'll give you a foundation for the rest of the book by explaining some basic information about financial terms and theories. In Part 3 you'll find advice for handling situations you are likely to face as you get started in your career, such as negotiating your salary, choosing your benefits, and building budgets. Part 4 looks at personal finance in the context of building a family: discussing money matters with your spouse, saving for college, and raising financially savvy kids. Part 5 covers saving for retirement, the ins and outs of Social Security, and what you need to know about long-term care. Finally, we'll wrap it all up with a brief word on contentment in Part 6.

Just in case the financial jargon gets a little too dry, I've also sprinkled some of my favorite stories and anecdotes, and my personal philosophy on investing throughout the book. Everything I know about money and confidence I learned in the context of my experiences, which is why I think the best way to learn about personal finance is to learn about it in the context of life—mine and yours. It's much more meaningful for me to discuss saving for your kids' college expenses by explaining how truly grateful I am that my parents saved for mine.

Likewise, I think it's more helpful to discuss budgeting and paying down debt in the context of what we want our lives to look like and what role money plays in that vision. I'm much more interested in examining how money affects all of life's messy, wonderful details than I am in discussing money in mathematical terms only. In fact, instead of categorizing this book as a personal finance book, let's categorize it as a book about life that includes discussions about personal finance. That sounds much more interesting anyway.

When I started out in the financial services industry, my boss shared something with me that has deeply influenced the way I view my work. He said money is a very intimate topic and talking about it with clients can be a very intimate experience, but an empathetic ear and a well-prepared plan can provide a great deal of peace and comfort. Money is a very intimate topic because it is uniquely tied to our feelings of safety and security. I know that personally—the thoughts that keep me up late at night are almost always linked to fear and anxiety. Fear of not having enough money to pay the bills provides a ton of fuel for anxiety. Talking about money opens the Pandora's box of "what ifs," and if we're honest with ourselves, most of us would rather not see those released into the open.

My desire is that this book will give you the tools you need to liberate yourself from the burdens of financial anxiety by teaching you how to approach the topics of money and investing with confidence. I hope this book will empower you to take charge of your money, instead of letting your money be in charge of you. Finally, I hope that you gain so much confidence regarding the financial areas of your life that it gushes over and spills into the rest of your life—because confidence is stunning and worth sharing with the world.

PART 1

Why It Matters

The greatest challenge for most of us is
believing that we are worthy now, right this minute.
Worthiness doesn't have prerequisites.

—BRENÉ BROWN, *THE GIFTS OF IMPERFECTION*

Before we get very deep into the financial details, I want to discuss why financial health matters in the first place. It's easy to sweep the topic of financial planning under the rug or to put it off for another more convenient time—which inevitably never comes. It takes a bit of effort to understand the fundamentals of finance and put that knowledge to work, but I believe it's worth the effort because you are worth the effort.

Part 1 is about valuing yourself enough to care about your finances and to deal with the things that often get in the way. In the first chapter we'll talk about why *you* matter and how understanding your worth should compel you to care for yourself in all areas of your life—including the financial ones. Then we'll dig into why talking about money is so hard and how to overcome some of those obstacles. Whether you feel ashamed about how little you have saved or you're concerned about keeping up with the Jones, you owe it to yourself and your future to get smart about your finances.

CHAPTER 1

You Matter

I HAVE A DEAR FRIEND who tells the best stories. She recently told me the most wonderful story that I want to share with you. Luckily, my friend is also a gifted writer, so all I had to do was copy and paste from her blog post. (I love when that happens.) In my opinion, her story about an angry parking lot encounter illustrates the central message we need to be telling ourselves when it comes to personal finance and life in general.

I had my blinker on to turn into a space when a car came zipping up. The driver, a pretty young woman, turned to look right at me as she was TAKING MY SPOT. Okay, maybe I was a teensy bit enraged. But I just shook my head and laughed, at which point she waved her middle finger at me and moved her mouth in loud-crazy-soundless-enraged-driver-with-the-windows-up voice and pulled right into the spot.

Mind you, this all took place in seconds. At 50 ... my reaction time was not very good, so I was just sitting there (with my blinker on) when she got out, slamming her door.

She looked over at me, noticed I was sitting there dumbstruck and still shaking my head, and took big, slightly stomping steps towards my car. I was mesmerized in the can't-look-away way. Remember, reaction time.

Also, she was so beautiful, a petite blonde probably in her early twenties, that her now multiple bird flipping was incongruously hilarious. She said "WHAT IS YOUR *expletives deleted* PROBLEM?!" Still, I stared. She got closer. "DID YOU HEAR ME?"

All I could think was "You are waaaaay too beautiful to act that way." She stood there glaring at me. I had to say something. Or I could have driven off. But remember, reaction time. So I said, "It's just that . . ."

"WHAT!"

"It's just that you're so beautiful."

"What?"

"I was just thinking that you are way too beautiful to act that way."

Stunned silence. But her posture mostly changed. She softened. "Well . . ." A little petulantly and mostly gratefully, "Thank you." And she backed away and went into the store.[2]

I love this story because it's all of us, and it's a reminder we all need. I have been that petite blond woman, believing myself to be entitled and glaring at a complete stranger for interrupting my air space. I have been my friend, completely blown away by someone cutting me off on the freeway or posting something nasty on social media. The world can be such an ugly place—a place where it's OK to curse at complete strangers in a Target parking lot.

The problem is, as my wonderful friend puts it, we have forgotten that we're beautiful. No one tells us, and it's often hard to remember. We live in a world full of media-inspired criticism. We're told from every side that we're not smart enough, thin enough, pretty enough, or successful enough; over time, the message wears us down. When we begin to believe it, we begin to behave as if it's true. But it isn't. We are all beautiful in our own unique way. We all matter—if for no other reason than we are humans, endowed with the ability to create, interact, and care for each other and ourselves.

You may be asking yourself what this little pep talk has to do with a book that is supposed to be about financial planning. It belongs here because I believe that you are worthwhile, that you are beautiful, and that you matter far too much to let money be a source of conflict in your life. In my opinion, our concept of our own self-worth has everything to do with financial planning because it has everything to do with living. In any venture, having a deep understanding of why you're doing what you're doing builds the foundation for your efforts and ultimately determines how successful you will be.

When I surveyed the financial services industry, my chosen field, I was incredibly disappointed at how little value it seems to place on women. I want to change that because I believe everyone is of great worth, so I wrote this book. My desire is to show women that they are valuable in the realm of personal finance and to empower them to succeed in that realm.

The Key to Achievement

I learned very early in my career that understanding and assigning *value* is essential to achieving success in money and in life. Understanding value is essential to getting along with others; it is essential to being successful in life, and it is essential to managing money. One of my favorite books about investing is *The Most Important Thing* by Howard

Marks, who, in my opinion, brilliantly lays out the importance of understanding the relationship between price and value. An investment opportunity is only as good as its price relative to what the investment is worth: its value. Something is valuable when it's in high demand, when it's desired by others.

Diamonds are valuable because people want them; they are desirable. Gold is valuable because it has so many commercial uses and because we have, as a culture, bestowed value upon it. Cupcakes are valuable because they are delicious, and I am willing to pay $6 for just one because it looks beautiful in the glass case at the local bakery.

But value is not bestowed only in the financial realm.

Having gobs of money does not make you worthy of love or security. Your life's value is not measured by how much wealth you can accumulate before you die. Nor do you have to spend your life focusing on financial checklists and spreadsheets. Although I believe in investing money wisely, I primarily want to invest in helping others realize that they are worthwhile so they can value themselves and the lives they have built.

When I asked my friend if I could reprint her story in my book, she responded, "Of course, but I'm curious about the application to a finance book." To me, her story is the crux of why I wanted to write this book. I want my readers to know that you are far too beautiful, far too smart, far too valuable, to neglect yourself. You are too beautiful to be flipping off someone in a parking lot, too beautiful not to treat your body right, too beautiful to be in a relationship with anyone who does not see your inner and outer beauty. You are far too beautiful not to do work that you believe in and that gives you purpose, too beautiful not to surround yourself with people who encourage and inspire you, too beautiful not to recognize your true value, too beautiful not to raise your fist to the sky and proclaim to the world: "I am stunning."

And you are far too beautiful to accept sloppy habits of spending and saving that will allow fears about your personal financial security to become a lifelong burden.

CHAPTER 2

Money Matters

MOST PEOPLE DON'T LIKE to talk about money, and the ones who do are usually awkward and uncomfortable to be around. The topic of money is a lot like politics and religion: you don't bring it up in polite company. When you meet someone new, you don't typically start a conversation by asking about the person's credit score or how much they earn. Unfortunately, this social discomfort too often makes most of us reluctant to talk about money even when we should.

I blame two attitudes for this unproductive reluctance to discuss money: our tendency to compare ourselves to others and our desire to avoid shame. Both can prevent us from taking charge of our finances. More important, they also rob us of joy, which is why I think we ought to address these attitudes head on. The tendency to compare ourselves to others and be ashamed about our own situation has always been there. However, I personally believe that the internet in general and social media in particular have magnified these problems.

I use social media to keep up with friends who live all over the country, but, truthfully, being on sites like Facebook often leaves me feeling empty at best and bad about myself at worst. As I scroll through picture after picture of seemingly perfect lives, I begin to feel more and more insecure. I wish I had the money to eat out as often as so and so does. I wish I could drive a car or wear clothing as nice as such and such's. So and so's home is straight out of Pinterest, and she is really good at taking pictures of it. My home is a mess right now, and when I try to take "artistic" pictures they always seem to come out blurry and with an orange tinge. What I see on the internet fuels discontent and makes me more keenly aware of what seems to be lacking in my own life. It keeps me from being grateful for what I have.

Talking about money can lead to similar results. As soon as I learn how much money someone earns, my mind immediately shifts to how much money I earn. Do I make more? Do I make less? If it's more, then I become prideful. If it's less, then I become jealous. I don't want to have those reactions. I want to be grateful that we are both employed and, hopefully, both doing things that we love and enjoy. I want to be content in the knowledge that there is a roof over my head and food on my table. And sometimes I am.

But then I hear that so and so just got into a prestigious master's program, and I start feeling sorry for myself again because my dreams of going back to school keep getting delayed. Unfortunately, there's nothing attractive about a pity party. I hope to someday be the type of person who can genuinely find joy in the success of others regardless of my own situation. In the meantime, I find it best to avoid making comparisons, which is a good move when it helps me to focus less on what we all own. But avoiding discussing money in every situation can be damaging if it causes me to avoid the conversations that could help me secure my financial future.

The Shame of Shame

Our fear of shame also makes it difficult to talk about money. A recent experience while traveling reminded me of the power of shame. The security line at the airport was moving slowly, so I left my husband with the bags and headed into what I thought was an empty X-ray machine. As I raised my arms, I heard a woman behind me mutter, "Who does she think she is, cutting in line like that? Some people are so utterly oblivious." As I realized I had accidentally cut in line, red-hot shame lit my face on fire. If I were the person I want to be, I would have turned and offered a simple apology. But I didn't. Instead, I hung my head and tried to sink into the ground. Then I spent the rest of the day replaying the scenario in my head and wallowing in my guilt.

Shame will do that to you. It will paralyze you. It will tell you that you're not enough and force you to use stupid excuses instead of doing the right thing. I hate shame. I think it is one of the greatest enemies of confidence.

In my time as an advisor, I've learned that shame is a significant factor in determining how we approach money and whether our approach is healthy or not. Whether it's shame over not having saved very much or shame over a failed financial venture, our shame can keep us from asking for help or looking for the best financial solutions. Interestingly enough, shame is often linked to comparisons. We feel ashamed when we haven't saved as much as our peers or when we haven't acquired the finer things in life that they own. Shame highlights our insufficiencies and shortcomings, making us feel worthless.

In her book *Daring Greatly*, author and shame researcher Brené Brown discusses how shame can be conquered. She writes, "If we can share our story with someone who responds with empathy and understanding, shame can't survive."[3] I 100 percent agree. It's important to realize that shame should not be ignored, much as we would prefer to. When I was younger and made poor decisions, my mother encouraged me to spend some time with my shame—to stare it in the face and learn from it. Only after that could I truly let it go. Our chance to live full lives can be hurt by both dwelling on our shame and also ignoring it altogether. Acknowledging shame and dealing with it allows us to learn from our failures and move on to better things.

In the context of your finances, dealing with your shame means that you must face your mistakes, learn from them, and move forward. Acknowledge your debt or your lack of savings. Go ahead and feel the burden of those problems and lean into how uncomfortable they are. If you ignore a problem, it will continue to grow, but when you really experience the discomfort, you're more likely to look for a solution.

Once you've acknowledged your failures, let them go. Don't let a past decision hang over your head for decades to come. Deal with it, but don't let it rule your life and deprive you of joy. There is so much more to living life than sitting around in the mud of our past mistakes. You are strong. Make the changes that need to be made and let go of the past so you can live free and unburdened by it. Then, move forward confidently.

The Importance of Trust

Our tendency to make unhealthy comparisons and our fear of shame are why it's so important that you find someone you can trust to help you with your finances. In 2007, Knowledge@Wharton, a research division of the University of Pennsylvania's business school, partnered with State Street

Global Advisors to study trust in the financial advisor-client relationship.[4] Not surprisingly, they found that trust is a key deciding factor when it comes to how individuals choose an advisor. More interesting, however, is how the researchers categorized types of trust. The first category discussed was trust in technical competence and know-how: do you trust that your advisor knows what he or she is doing? The second category was trust in ethical conduct and character: do you trust that your advisor is honest?

The final category in the study was trust in empathetic skills and maturity. Dr. James Grubman, a psychologist who specializes in training financial professionals, explains:

This level of trust, which we might call relationship competence, may be the most critical because without it, the relationship is extremely fragile. Essentially, this trust is built on the client's premise that "if I tell you personal things about myself or my family, I need to trust that you, the advisor, will handle that well."

The more meetings I have with clients and potential clients, the more I believe this to be true. Talking about your finances is a very intimate and personal experience, and seeing how advisors respond to that information dictates how well you, as a client, can trust them. In my personal experience, this type of trust is particularly important for women. Studies show that women are often more empathetic than men, making this category of trust that much more important for us.[5] When we bring something as intimate as our finances—which are really just vessels for our hopes and dreams—to the table, we need to be met with sincere empathy, genuine kindness, and understanding. That's why you should look for those traits in a financial advisor. Obviously, you want the advisor to be competent as well—and we'll discuss how to determine that later in the book—but you must first be able to trust them with your story.

Now that we've dealt with the issues of shame and comparisons, it's time to hunker down and talk about money. The more we talk about it, the easier it will get. There are things in life that have a great deal of power over us until we speak them out loud. Over and over again in client meetings, I've watched as a wave of relief washes over an individual who finally has the opportunity to safely say out loud, "This is an area of my life that is keeping me up at night, and I want to change that."

I hope that as you read this book, you find the courage to speak out loud about things in your life that need to be addressed, particularly in regard to your finances. Maybe that means having a difficult conversation with your family about your will. Maybe it means creating a will in the first place. Maybe it means speaking about your debt to a confidant or an advisor. Simply acknowledging problems is a huge first step. Once you've acknowledged them, you can begin to tackle them and change your circumstances for the better.

PART 2

Fundamentals of Finance

Give a girl an education, and introduce her properly into the world, and ten to one, she has the means of settling well, without further expense to anybody.

—JANE AUSTEN, *MANSFIELD PARK*

In his 2002 letter to Berkshire Hathaway stockholders, Warren Buffet noted that "it's not until the tide goes out that you find out who's been swimming naked."[6] It's a funny image but also a very sobering observation. Buffett's folksy allegory means that when the market is going up, every investing strategy looks good. It's only during major downturns that you find out who has been making poor decisions—"swimming naked." Part 2 aims to help you understand the fundamentals of finance so that you'll be less likely to be exposed if the financial tide goes out.

If you haven't figured this out yet, I love dessert. I also really enjoy baking. Throughout this book, I use a lot of baking analogies. I think describing finance in kitchen terms can help reduce the intimidation factor and clarify some tricky concepts. Consider Part 2 your tour around a well-stocked kitchen—you need to know the names of some of the basic equipment and ingredients before you pick up an unfamiliar recipe. These chapters won't make you an expert in finance (or a top-notch chef, which I am sadly not), and they should not be considered a substitute for professional advice, but they will offer explanations of the basics—stocks and bonds, fees, and taxes.

You're not going to find some of the fanciest tools here; there are no discussions of derivatives, futures, or real estate investing. That's because my goal is to show you just enough so you can choose wisely when you look for help in managing your money, and so you can hold those people accountable for the services they provide you. If you'd like to go beyond the basics offered here, I suggest that you check out the CFA® Institute's blog *The Enterprising Investor*, which is, in my opinion, an excellent source for investing information put together by a well-established, highly esteemed organization.

CHAPTER 3

Financial Lingo

WRITING THIS SECTION was a violent struggle. I expect that by the time you read it, I will have rewritten it twenty times or more. When my mom read an early draft of the book, she asked if I could make this section less boring—which tells you something about the nature of my struggle and also my relationship with my mom. But I can't write a book about personal finance without offering you some semblance of an understanding of basic financial markets and investing.

I love finance. I love finance like I love dessert. For me, finance is a constantly moving puzzle that I'm forever trying to piece together, and for whatever demented reason I really enjoy that. Of course, most people hate it, which is why you're going to be tempted to skip this section of the book. But please don't! Finance may be a confusing and not terribly exciting topic, but don't let that intimidate you. Because the less you understand, the easier it can be for some less-than-ethical types to trick you into making poor financial decisions.

I am passionate about preventing that kind of deception. I believe an informed woman is an empowered woman. That's why I'm going to lay out the financial fundamentals I think you need to understand to make good financial decisions in every stage of your life. I promise I will make it as lively as possible.

The Conundrum of Wise Investing

I am a skeptical investor, which probably sounds weird coming from a financial advisor. Don't get me wrong—I definitely believe that you *should* invest. But I am skeptical that the best investment decisions can be made quickly or easily. It makes me nervous to see how willingly some people hand over their money. You need to think long and hard before investing in something. I fear that most people make snap judgments simply because they don't have enough information to make good ones. To make wise investments, it helps to know some basics about the financial markets.

The media and entertainment industry have portrayed financial markets as some kind of half-glamorous, half-corrupt, *Wolf of Wall Street,* casino experience. They aren't. In reality, the financial markets are intended to allocate resources (money) to the right places—the most efficient places. That is why they were created. A long time ago someone thought, "Wouldn't it be great if growing companies could have access to more money so that they could grow even more? They would have to pay a fee for borrowing that money (interest), but if they are a good company and use that money to grow, then they can pay back whatever they borrowed and everyone would be better off." Then it magically happened and *voila:* capitalism (this description is oversimplified and historically inaccurate, but it's good enough for our purposes here).

It's oversimplified, but it's accurate to say that the goal

of the financial markets is to connect people who have extra cash and want to make more money off of that cash with companies that need extra cash in order to grow. The extra-cash people put some of their money to work with the need-cash companies, which use the extra funds to do more research, create better products, provide more jobs, and ultimately grow bigger. When the process works the way it's supposed to, the need-cash company makes more money, the extra-cash people who invested in the company make more money than they invested, the company makes better products, hires more people, and everyone ends up better off. Yay!

But what about the Great Depression, you ask? What about the financial crisis of 2008? What about the volatility of the financial markets? Ahhhh, yes. For better or for worse, underlying all great institutions are people, and people are imperfect. Behind all the graphs and red and green arrows are people: people making trades, people selling financial products, people trying to make money. Sometimes people make mistakes that hurt their companies, which in turn hurts their investors and the markets overall.

Sometimes people get greedy and do deceitful things, and that can hurt the rest of us who are trying to use the same system honestly. That is essentially what happened in 2008. Instead of investing in good, healthy, growing companies that would be able to pay back the money invested in them, too many people started investing in mortgages. And it turns out, a lot of those mortgages were given to people who couldn't pay them back. Things got really complicated. A lot of people in a lot of institutions failed to do the right thing, and eventually the housing bubble popped. For a time, things were a real mess.

Fortunately, the story doesn't end there. The markets were resilient. They recovered in spades. But some tough things had to happen first. Companies went under, people lost their homes, their jobs, and their retirement savings. But slowly, we were able to heal and rebuild. That is the beauty of the financial markets. When they function as they were intended, money gets shifted around until it ends up in the right places once again—places that include opportunity for growth.

I prefer to approach the markets like I approach my cat. I expect it to be a positive experience, but I approach her cautiously lest my timing is wrong—because that's usually when she will scratch the living daylights out of me. The financial markets really can be a good thing. They allow companies like Google and Apple to flourish, enabling them to make great products that make our lives better. We simply need to be cautious and mindful that the markets are made up of imperfect people who sometimes get greedy and mess things up.

What You Need to Know!

As I mentioned previously, I was a wreck writing this chapter. I wanted to tell you everything I know about this subject because I think it's fascinating and I love it all so much. Luckily for you, I ultimately realized that the most beneficial thing for you to know is the basics—enough to ask good questions and not be misled. Of course, if you want to know more, I'll be happy to point you to some more in-depth sources (and you can find my contact info at the back of this book).

My personal rule of thumb is not to invest in anything I don't 100 percent understand. If I don't understand how an investment product works, there's a much greater risk that someone could take advantage of me, so I choose to avoid those situations altogether. That might be a harder rule for you to follow if you don't have a background in finance. Don't worry. I'm about to explain some of the most common financial tools and vocabulary by comparing them to baked goods, which will not only help you make basic financial decisions but may also make you start looking for the nearest bakery.

What Is a Stock?

Stocks are the cupcakes of the financial world. They form the core of most individual portfolios, are what most people think of first when they consider investing, and are often portrayed as sexy and glamorous in terrible movies about stockbrokers. Stocks are also known as *equities.* When people say they own *shares* of Apple, they are talking about stocks.

The key word with stocks is "own." When you buy one share of Apple stock, you become the proud owner of a teeny tiny slice of Apple's pie. Because you own a slice of Apple, you can now participate in Apple's profits. When Apple does well, you make money. When Apple does poorly, you lose money. There's a bunch of other nifty stuff I could teach you about stocks, but according to my mother, it's boring, so we'll stop here.

What you need to remember: stocks = ownership.

What Is a Bond?

If stocks are the cupcakes of the financial world, bonds are the muffins. Bonds are also known as *fixed-income vehicles.* They can be as bland as bran muffins or as weird and confusing as pistachio-chai muffins. While the bond universe is much bigger than the stock universe, bonds are much more complex and not as glamorous, so they don't get as much attention.

The key word with bonds is "loan." When you buy a bond, you are actually loaning a bit of money to a company, and the bond functions as an IOU. When you buy a bond from Apple you do not get a share of the company in exchange for your money. Instead, you lend Apple money, and Apple agrees to pay you interest during the life of the bond and then give you back the money you spent on the bond when it comes due.

Bonds are considered conservative investments, and they should be a part of most investment portfolios. Bonds have priority over stocks when it comes to bankruptcy, so if a company goes belly up, bondholders get paid back before stockholders, who sometimes don't get their money back at all. This makes bonds a much safer investment. Additionally, you can buy bonds from the U.S. government, which are considered the safest investment in the world because—so far—the U.S. government has not gone belly up, and few people believe it ever will.

What you need to remember: bonds = lending

What Is a Mutual Fund?

Mutual funds are collections of stocks, bonds, and other more complicated types of investment vehicles. Most people have heard of mutual funds because they are one of the more common forms of investments. If you have the option to invest in a 401(k) or something like it through your workplace, mutual funds will most likely be the type of investment vehicle offered to you.

I find it easiest to think of a mutual fund as a pizza (technically not a baked good, but equally delicious). Let's say you're a poor college student with a hankering for some pizza—you're not interested in individual portions of pepperoni or cheese or marinara sauce—you want a pizza that includes all of those ingredients. Unfortunately, you can't afford to buy a whole pizza for yourself, but your roommates are also hungry for pizza, so you combine your money and call for a delivery. By purchasing the pizza together, you can now each have a slice with all of the ingredients. Yum!

A mutual fund takes money from a bunch of people, pools it together, buys a bunch of individual stocks, bonds, or both, combines them into a financial pizza, and gives you back a slice of the whole pie. Mutual funds allow you to get some "ingredients" that you probably couldn't afford if you tried to buy them separately. Some stocks are really expensive, which makes it difficult to purchase very many of them without a large sum of cash. A share of Apple's stock (at the time of this writing) trades at around $100. That's a lot of money for just one share.

If you only have a few hundred dollars to invest, then you can only buy a few stocks from a few companies. If one of those companies tanks, then you are likely to lose all the money you invested there. In finance-speak we call this "market exposure." Exposure is the percent of your portfolio invested in a particular type of investment vehicle (also known as a security), region of the world, industry, or index. Your best bet is to invest so that you have exposure to a lot of companies and industries, something we call "diversification," and which I'll explain further below. But it's hard to diversify if you can only afford to buy a few stocks or bonds.

That's where mutual funds come in. When you buy shares of a mutual fund, you invest in a bunch of different companies, without having to research all of the "ingredients" yourself. For example, you can get a share of Vanguard's *Total Stock Market Index Fund* for around $50 at the time of this writing, which consequently allows you to invest in (you guessed it) the entire stock market—as defined by Vanguard.

Mutual funds might have really bizarre sounding names like *Balance Wealth Strategy A*, *International Strategic Core C*, or *Fire Breathing Unicorn Total Return D*, which is what I will call my fund as soon as my boss, Steve, gives me the chance to prove my investing prowess. The name of the fund is also represented by a ticker symbol, which is a combination of five letters (sometimes more if there are multiple versions of the fund) that allows you to easily search for the fund from places like finance.google.com.

These days you can find a mutual fund that combines almost every ingredient under the sun—just like pizzas in a fusion restaurant. Some are funds that include a sampling of particular industries or from the same regions in the world or from companies that are small or large or medium-sized. Some are called index funds because they will give you exposure to all the stocks in a particular listing of certain types of companies, such as the S&P 500 (the 500 largest companies in the US) or the Dow Jones Index (a collection of large companies initially chosen by Charles Dow and now compiled by the S&P Dow Jones Indices). There are mutual funds for bonds, mutual funds full of fancy derivatives, mutual funds built to help you retire, and many more. But all you really need to know is that mutual funds give you a slice of that multi-ingredient pizza.

One other helpful thing to note: mutual funds record their price at the end of the day. This is different from stocks and other securities that "price" all day long. This means there will be only one price for a mutual fund each day, and it will represent the worth of the total contents of the fund when the market closes. Regardless of whether you put in your order before breakfast or at your afternoon snack break, you will pay the same price for a mutual fund share.

What Is an ETF?

An ETF is a lot like a younger, more hip mutual fund. It also has some elements of a stock built into it, so think of it as the love child of a mutual fund and a stock—or maybe a pizza cupcake. ETF stands for exchange traded fund. The exchange traded part is what makes it similar to a stock. Unlike mutual funds, which price at the end of the day, ETFs price all day long, which means you can trade them much like you trade stocks. You can buy them at one price early in the day and sell them for another price in the afternoon.

ETFs are like mutual funds because they also provide you with the option of purchasing a piece of the pie. ETFs are cheap and flexible. They're easy to trade and usually cost less than mutual funds because most of them are index funds, which (remember) are funds that invest in the stocks or bonds included in a pre-existing index. The objective of an index fund is already laid out; it is expected to match the index—which means the fund should include shares of all firms represented in the index. That objective makes it a lot easier for fund managers to run an index fund because it requires less research and thereby fewer hours than an actively managed fund—one that is built and continually traded by a fund manager. Because index funds are cheaper to maintain, the savings are passed on to you in the form of lower fees.

A Word about Cash

You may be feeling overwhelmed at this point. There's so much out there to invest in, why not just leave your money in cash and avoid the headache? Well, frankly, because that is one of the riskiest options out there. There was a time when leaving your money in a bank savings account could earn you a decent amount from the interest, but that is no longer the case. Today, a savings account at Bank of America is likely to earn you less than 1 percent annually.[7] When you consider the fact that inflation—the amount that the cost of living goes up each year—increases by about 3 percent each year, you can see how this becomes a problem.

Over time your chunk of change at the bank will buy you less and less as things cost more and more. You don't have to put your money in the stock market, but you should invest it in something with a risk profile that you can stomach and that meets your needs. Furthermore, it's incredibly difficult to predict when the market will fall and when it will rise, which is why it's a good idea to average into the market by investing a little bit of your money in pieces over time.

Building a Smart Portfolio
Diversification

One of the primary tenants of smart investing is the concept of diversification, which essentially calls for not putting all of your eggs into one basket. The basic idea here is that by spreading out your exposure to more than one company, you don't have to worry so much about picking a "winner" because you will lose less if one company tanks. If you invest 100 percent of your money in one stock and that stock falls 50 percent you lose half of your money, but if you invest your money in twenty stocks and one stock falls 50 percent you only lose 2.5 percent of your money.

By diversifying your investments, you set yourself up for a much smoother ride that's less likely to create the panic and fear that leads to poor decision-making. I'll be honest here: you will probably never become an investing millionaire this way. Getting to that level requires making big bets, but most people can't stomach that type of investing because it is in essence just that—betting.

Instead, it's a good idea to spread your exposure across different types of companies (big, medium, and small), and different parts of the world (domestic and international). It's also a good idea to split your money between the aggressive stock market and the more conservative bond market because the two have historically had an inverse relationship to one another (though not always). This means that when the stock market rises, the bond market usually falls, and when the stock market struggles, bonds typically do better. If you're invested in both, the result is a less volatile graph of your investment returns.

Asset Allocation
Asset allocation has to do with how you allocate your assets (your money) to different investments. Let's say you have $100,000 to invest. You invest $50,000 in the stock market, $45,000 in the bond market, and leave $5,000 in cash for emergencies. Your asset allocation is 50 percent stocks, 45 percent bonds, and 5 percent cash.

Target Date Funds
Target date funds are essentially funds that shift their asset allocation from aggressive (more stocks) to conservative

(more bonds) as you approach retirement. While they do have some downsides, which I'll discuss later, the concept behind them is actually quite economically sound.

As an investor you have both human capital and financial capital. Human capital is essentially your ability to earn money. Financial capital is already earned money that you have saved up. At the beginning of your career, you are at your highest level of human capital because you have the greatest potential to earn money (the rest of your career) and your lowest level of financial capital—unless you are lucky enough to have inherited money. As you near retirement, your human capital decreases because you have fewer and fewer years to earn money, but your financial capital is hopefully at its peak—meaning your savings are the highest they've ever been. Thus, the two types of capital largely have an inverse relationship for most individuals—again excepting those who have inherited money at a young age.

These two types of capital can be thought of as two types of assets, each with its own set of risks. The risk to human capital is that you may be fired or disabled while working, in which case you wouldn't be able to work and would need to live off of your financial capital—your savings. The risk to financial savings is that it won't last as long as you need it to. These are both very real risks and should be hedged accordingly. To hedge the risk to human capital, it's important to be saving and, in some instances, you may want to consider insurance, which we'll discuss later. To hedge the risks to financial capital, you need to balance how much you have saved against your ability to keep working. This is where the target date concept comes in.

At the onset of your career you have a lot of human capital. If something happens in the market you have plenty of time to recoup your losses, which puts you in a position to be more "aggressive" with your investments. Being aggressive with your investments doesn't mean you throw your money around angrily; it means that you can make riskier investments, which have the potential to both make and lose more of your money. As you approach retirement and your human capital decreases, you have less time to recoup losses from catastrophic events, so you should adjust your portfolio to be more conservative, which means your investments carry less potential for spectacular gains but also less risk of huge losses.

Because target date funds slowly adjust their allocation over time, at first glance they appear to be a surefire way to provide for adjusting your investment risk as you get older. However, target date funds are a lot like automated assembly lines—they work great for the basics but aren't easily adjusted for specific scenarios. If something unexpected were to occur, the target date fund is not going to adjust. Likewise, target date funds don't consider your whole situation, but rather only basic variables such as your current age and years until retirement. When it comes to the risks associated with your ability to earn money and to comfortably retire, the ideal portfolio is one that matches the split between aggressive and conservative investments, while also taking other factors, such as insurance, into account.

Types of Fees
Fees are a crucial part of how well your investments perform, which means it's worth your while to understand exactly what fees you're paying to invest your money, when you're paying them, and how they are being charged to you.

Management Fees

These are the fees that you pay to your advisor, and they should be the easiest to understand and keep track of. Advisors should tell you up front exactly what they charge—whether that is a flat annual fee or a percent of assets charged at certain intervals (quarterly, semi-annually, annually). Fee details should be noted in your contract with your advisor. Because management fees are likely some of the larger fees you'll pay, you should give them considerable scrutiny. The difference between paying 1 percent and 2 percent on your assets may not feel like much, but over time the difference can be significant. If you're paying 2 percent or more for professional management of your assets, your advisor should be doing an *exceptional* job for you. If they're not, it may be time to look elsewhere.

Trading Fees

We often forget about trading fees when we're not actively involved in managing our own portfolios, but they play an important role in performance. Typically, custodians such as Schwab, Fidelity, E-Trade, etc., charge a fee for trading most funds and stocks.

For example, if that fee is $25, every time your advisor adds a new fund to your portfolio, you pay $25. To make room for the new fund, your advisor may also sell an old fund, which costs you another $25. If your advisor makes twenty trades in a year, you're paying $500 a year in trading fees alone.

Fund Fees

In addition to the fees your advisor charges and the fees you pay to trade, the manager of any fund you invest in also takes a bite off the top in the form of a fund fee. Unlike management and trading fees, which should both be available for you to view, fund fees are much harder to see because they're charged net of the fund's performance. So, if the manager of your fund made you 7 percent this year, you may only see 6 percent when you look at your performance records because the manager took 1 percent (or more or less depending on what they choose to charge).

Ask your advisor about fund fees. A good advisor should be mindful of what fees are being charged by the funds they're choosing for your portfolio and should consider if the fund's performance justifies its fee. As I previously mentioned, funds that follow an index typically have a much lower fee, making them cheaper alternatives.

Commissions

Commissions are a type of fee charged by brokers. As a Registered Investment Advisor, my firm and others like it do not charge commissions because we serve as an alternative to a broker for our clients. However, it's important to recognize that brokers are compensated for what they sell in the form of commissions, which can consequently misalign their interests and yours.

Types of Taxes

We rarely call them fees, but taxes can also be considered a type of fee on your account. A good financial advisor should be mindful of the impact of taxes and pursue a tax-efficient strategy that helps maximize returns and minimize taxes, leaving you with more in your account at the end of the day.

There are three main forms of taxes when it comes to investing: long-term capital gains, short-term capital gains, and ordinary income. Capital gains occur when the amount in your account after a sale is larger than the amount that was there before the sale. The sale is important because it "recognizes" the gains or losses in your account. As long as the investment position is unsold, your gain is unrealized and nothing happens. When your ending amount after a sale is smaller than your beginning amount, you have a loss, and the government does not make you pay taxes when you lose money. In fact, the IRS will allow you to use your losses to cancel out your gains. How nice of them!

Long-Term Capital Gains

Long-term capital gains are gains that occurred over more than a year. The best thing to have tax-wise is losses because losses = no taxes. Of course, losses also mean you didn't make any money so there is a trade-off there. The second-best thing to have is long-term capital gains because the tax rate is the lowest for this type of gain. The government incentivizes long-term gains over short-term gains to discourage people from creating chaos in the market by constantly trading in and out of stocks or funds. The amount of taxes you pay on your long-term gains is linked to your income, ranging from 0 percent for those in lower tax brackets to 20 percent for those in higher tax brackets.[8] Keep in mind that the tax is levied only on the gain and not on the entire sale, meaning if in January of 2016 you bought a stock for $50 and in February of 2017 you sold the stock for $55 you will pay taxes only on the $5 gain, not on the total $55 proceeds of the sale.

Short-Term Capital Gains

Short-term capital gains are gains realized in less than a year—meaning that in less than a year you bought and sold something that made money. Short-term capital gains are taxed at your ordinary income tax rate, which is higher than the long-term capital gains rates and makes them less desirable. If you pay 28 percent on your income in taxes, then you will also pay 28 percent on short-term gains.

Food for Thought

Before we discuss how dividends are taxed, we need to define what a dividend is. When a company is doing well it may want to distribute a portion of its earnings to its shareholders (stock owning investors). It does this by paying a dividend either in the form of a cash payment or shares of stock. It's important to note that in a vacuum, a dividend payout decreases a stock's price by the amount of the payout; however, this is difficult to observe in reality because the stock price is always moving.

Qualified Dividends

Qualified dividends are taxed at the same rate as long-term capital gains. In order for dividends to be qualified, they must be paid by a U.S. corporation or qualified foreign corporation, meet the holding period requirements (sixty days during the 121-day period that covers sixty days before and sixty days after the ex-dividend date), and not meet any of the IRS exclusion criteria. That's a lot of boring rules. Luckily, the financial statement that your custodian and/

or advisor sends you around tax time will tell you which kind of dividends you've received. Great!

Food for Thought

Your advisor can employ other strategies such as tax-loss harvesting that take advantage of losses to minimize your taxes while still pursuing the overarching objective of making you money. Make sure to discuss your tax situation with your advisor and ask them how they pursue a tax-efficient investment strategy.

Nonqualified Dividends

Nonqualified dividends are just like they sound: dividends that are not qualified for tax exemption. Nonqualified dividends are taxed at the same rate as your ordinary income, just like short-term capital gains are.

CHAPTER 4

Finance and
Your Feelings

THE LAST CHAPTER was all about facts. This one is about feelings. There are times when investing in the financial markets can feel like an emotional rollercoaster. When things are going well and you're making money, you feel great. But out of nowhere the markets can drop, and you suddenly find yourself curled up on the floor, clutching your tummy and crying out, "Make it stop!" You may respond by impulsively selling out of all of your accounts or eating an entire carton of ice cream, but neither action will actually make you feel any better. The pain is still there, and actually, you may have just made it worse.

That's why I'm devoting this chapter to a concept called *behavioral finance*. The field of behavioral finance is relatively new and still gaining traction, but I believe it is crucially important that you understand the concepts behind behavioral finance in order to become and remain financially stable.

In the past few years, economists have realized that people's emotions play a much bigger role in the financial markets than they had previously thought. Most human beings (we're not talking about traditional economists here) are not robots. They are emotional beings who respond to things that happen around them in emotional ways. These emotional responses, while completely genuine, have been the greatest downfall of many investors over the years. Our emotions cause us to do crazy things. When we're in pain we act impulsively, and impulsive decisions are rarely good ones.

The solution, in my humble semi-professional opinion, is to acknowledge that emotions do play a role in our investing decisions. Instead of trying to ignore those emotions, we must allow them to be a part of the way we invest. We feel what we feel. Our emotions are a part of our most authentic selves, and pretending they don't exist can be detrimental to our health. At the same time, letting our emotions run unchecked in our lives can also be unhealthy, particularly when it comes to our financial well-being.

Instead, we should do our best to be aware of where we're emotionally vulnerable and be mindful of what we can do to combat impulsive financial decision-making. The remainder of this chapter is taken from a series of articles I wrote on the topic of behavioral finance for my firm's website (www. cedarstoneadvisors.com). I am very passionate about behavioral finance because it combines my love of finance and my fascination with people and how their minds work. I think you will find these ideas helpful the next time you start relying on your emotions when making monetary decisions.

The Rational Economic Woman

The idea of the "rational economic man" first appeared in the late nineteenth century and has been referred to by a variety of economists and economic theories since then. Because this is a book for women, we will henceforth refer to the superior decision-maker for this topic: the "rational economic woman."

The rational economic woman is, in many ways, the biggest nerd. She makes decisions based on optimal utility—the greatest reward for the least amount of risk. She is perfectly rational, perfectly self-interested, and she has all the information there is to have. When the rational economic woman decides it's time to buy a car, she really does buy the best one on the market for the best price. She does all of this through the use of mathematical equations that allow her to calculate the best option at all times.

Contrary to the rational economic woman, there is the "dramatic woman." She is a busybody who likes to make fiery, passionate claims with little appreciation for the truth or for rational argument. When she decides it's time to buy a car, she will make her choice based on color and cupholders with no thought about gas mileage or resale value.

It is my personal opinion that most of us fall somewhere in between these two women. I for one do not make complex mathematical calculations when deciding what to have for breakfast. I also try not to make dramatic, sweeping statements that may or may not be true. Living by emotions alone is an easy way to offend individuals and lose friends. It's also one of the easiest ways to lose money when it comes to the financial markets.

The rational economic man was dreamed up to help economists make sense of the way the markets work. This fictional man is part of the broader topic of traditional finance, which covers most of the subject's fundamental theories and equations. However, the field of behavioral finance in recent years has begun to challenge some of the theories of traditional finance, arguing that most individuals aren't perfectly rational and that the markets don't actually operate under the assumption that all information is equally available to everyone. In reality, fear and greed do play a role in the markets, and emotions cannot simply be ignored when it comes to investing.

Accounting for Feelings

You can't help but feel the way you feel; however, when we begin to make investing decisions based on our emotions, we are likely to find ourselves making poor decisions. Emotions lead us to sell out at the bottom or to assume that we should purchase a company's stock simply because we like that company's product. It's also silly to assume that we can completely remove emotions from the markets. As long as people are behind buys and sells, the markets will rise and fall, at least in part, due to human behavior.

One of the key attributes of a quality financial advisor is someone who understands that who you are should play a role in how you invest. Too many advisors want to ask questions only about how to invest your funds. In reality, they should be asking questions about your goals and your fears.

As the study of behavioral finance gains credibility, more and more research is showing us how to incorporate risk-tolerance levels with investing and how to avoid unnecessary expenses from over-trading. We are learning how to use tools that help us identify our emotional strengths and weaknesses, which puts us in a much better place to combat irrational decision-making. My goal in the remainder of this chapter is to help you:

- identify certain biases regarding the markets;
- understand some of the key assumptions that underlie the market; and

- see where these assumptions fall short and what you can do to bridge the gap.

The big difference between traditional finance and behavioral finance is a question of what *should* happen (traditional) versus what *actually* happens (behavioral). It is, in many ways, analogous to predicting the weather. In the morning, we wake up and turn on our television and the weather forecaster tells us what to expect of the day's weather based on all of the signs and data collected by the meteorology center at your local news station. At the end of the day, you turn on the evening news and hear the weather forecaster explain what weather your area actually experienced. As science and technology has improved over the years, meteorologists have gotten more and more accurate at predicting the weather, but it remains an imperfect art. The study of traditional and behavioral finance, too, remains imperfect although it continues to improve.

Efficient Market Hypothesis

Traditional finance is predicated on a theory known as the efficient market hypothesis. Developed by economist Eugene Fama, it basically says that investors should never be able to beat (outsmart) the market because the market reflects all available information; it is efficient. If we assume the world is made up entirely of little rational economic men and women making perfect decisions based on perfect information, then we can also assume that the financial market operates with perfect efficiency and the best return we can earn is that of the market. Of course, if we assume that everyone is *not* rational, we would conclude that the market is not *perfectly* efficient.

Consider a story by Malcolm Gladwell that was published

in the *New Yorker* in 2007.[9] The story, "Open Secrets," discusses the Enron scandal and ends with a short paragraph about a group of Cornell University students who did a term project on Enron in the spring of 1998. In the course of their research, the group concluded that Enron was engaging in a very risky strategy and "may be manipulating its earnings." Gladwell noted that the information was published on Cornell's business school website and remained there for many years. The information was there, yet investors completely missed it!

Many similar stories prove to us that the markets aren't perfectly efficient. So we have to be alert not only to our own decision-making but also to the decision-making of others and to what's going on in the world around us.

Food for Thought

The markets may operate efficiently most of the time, but discrepancies remain. In addition, some markets are less efficient than others because information about them is harder to come by. Approach the markets cautiously and be mindful of your own shortcomings when it comes to investing.

When the Truth Hurts: Cognitive and Emotional Biases

There are two major types of behavioral biases: cognitive errors and emotional biases. Cognitive errors are the result of cognitive dissonance, which can be thought of as the discomfort you feel when something contradicts your beliefs. For example, let's say that I personally believe that cupcakes are good for you and a healthy alternative to carrots, but one day I come across an article that points out that cupcakes are loaded with sugar and carbs and will go straight to my thighs if I eat them. This creates a dissonance in my thinking: I believe that cupcakes are good for me, but there is evidence that strongly contradicts my beliefs.

Cognitive Biases

Understanding cognitive dissonance is important because it has significant implications for the way we make decisions. Consider a few types of biases that can be labeled cognitive errors; in the list below, I name the bias, define it, and provide an example.[10]

- **Conservatism:** *A bias in which people maintain their prior views or forecasts by inadequately incorporating new information.* For example: Despite reading the contradictory article, I can continue to believe that cupcakes will help me lose weight and give me a beautiful complexion by choosing to selectively accept or reject the scientific research in a way that will support my ideas.
- **Confirmation:** *A bias in which people tend to look for and notice information that confirms what they believe but ignore information that contradicts what they believe.* For example: I may search only for articles that tout the health benefits of cupcakes and ignore anything that says otherwise.
- **Illusion of control:** *A bias in which people tend to believe they can control or influence outcomes when they can't.* For example: I may believe that by making my cupcakes with low-fat ingredients I can force them to become healthy.

- **Hindsight bias:** *A bias in which people may see past events as having been predictable and reasonable to expect.* For example: After having eaten a whole tray of cupcakes, I announce that I knew it would make me feel terrible but that it was a reasonable outcome to expect because the healthy activity of working out also makes me feel terrible.

These biases are common—not just in finance but in everyday life. I would posit that they're so common because it is very difficult for us as humans to admit that we are wrong or that events aren't as predictable as we would like them to be.

Unfortunately, ignoring the presence and impact of cognitive errors is very dangerous. In investing, as in life, when we fail to consider uncomfortable alternatives, we put ourselves at risk of not making fully-informed decisions. One of the worst things I can do for my clients is fail to consider new information simply because I'm more comfortable clinging to my initial views or because I don't want to admit that I might have been wrong.

We often see cognitive errors at work when an individual is involved in the success of a company. Their investment becomes personal and their self-worth ends up tied to the outcome of a stock, which causes them to behave irrationally. They want to be right more than they want to be smart, so they seek out information that confirms their beliefs and ignore anything that contradicts them. If they end up being right, they say, "I knew it all along." If they end up being wrong, they blame someone or something else for their failure. Instead of investing based on facts, they are investing based on feelings, and that is a dangerous road to travel.

The best weapon we have against making cognitive errors is to seek out information that contradicts our beliefs and make an unbiased effort to reconcile the new information with our beliefs. To help me rationally investigate the health benefits of cupcakes, I should make friends with people who think differently than I do (like my husband who thinks dessert is evil) and consider their contrary opinions and the evidence behind those opinions. We don't know what we don't know, but we can help ourselves by considering all angles of a decision—not just the one that is most comfortable or makes us feel best.

Emotional Biases

Unlike cognitive errors, which result from faulty reasoning, emotional biases result from our preconceived attitudes and feelings, and that makes them even harder to correct. They are also more dangerous than cognitive biases because they can lead to impulsive decisions that can have significant consequences. If you're concerned that your emotions are getting the best of you when it comes to your money, consider some of the following biases and ask yourself if any of them sound uncomfortably familiar.[11]

- **Overconfidence bias:** A *bias in which investors have a higher than warranted faith in their own abilities.* For example: Most people will say they are above-average drivers. A surprising number of individuals will also say they saw the stock market crash of 2008 coming. The former is statistically impossible, and the second is highly unlikely. Both imply that individuals have a tendency to think very highly of their abilities. When it comes to investing, this can result in unwarranted risk-taking that can have devastating consequences.

- **Regret-aversion bias:** *A bias in which investors tend to avoid decisions and actions out of fear that they will have poor results.* For example: My husband and I recently planned a trip to Ireland. On Black Friday we found incredible prices for roundtrip airfare but we didn't buy the tickets because we weren't fully committed to the trip. By the time we had fully decided to buy the tickets, the price had doubled. To this day my husband regrets not buying those tickets and brings it up whenever we think about planning another trip. For investors, this looks like failing to buy into a down market because they fear it will continue to fall, causing them pain and regret for their decision. However, what often ends up happening is that the investor, paralyzed by fear, misses out on the eventual upswing as well. Because regret-aversion is so powerful, it is crucial that we have a disciplined approach to investing so that our decisions will be driven by rational thought processes and data instead of fear of regret.

- **Status quo bias:** *A bias in which investors choose to do nothing, thereby maintaining the status quo as opposed to making a change that may be beneficial in the long run.* For example: I went to the same hairdresser to get my hair cut for a long time, even though I knew I could get a better hair cut for less money elsewhere. Although I was unhappy with my hairdresser, I felt an emotional pull not to change my routine. For investors, this emotional bias can lead to a very poorly constructed portfolio because it keeps them from selling poorly performing assets and/or diversifying across other asset classes. It can also be a detriment to individuals when it comes to financial planning. The inability to seek out other information and advice out of a sense of loyalty or fear of change can be incredibly harmful if it means getting bad advice or no advice at all.

Education is key to overcoming emotional biases. The more you know and the more you question your assumptions and decisions, the less likely you are to make impulsive, emotional decisions that can hurt you financially. When it comes to investing, it's always good to have a healthy dose of skepticism and to be aware of how your emotions affect your decision-making.

CHAPTER 5

Finding the Right Financial Advisor

I've thrown a lot of information at you in the last couple of chapters. I hope it has given you a better understanding of some of the most basic tools and theories of investing—without completely overwhelming you! I wouldn't be surprised, though, if you've started thinking about finding a professional financial advisor to help you navigate the world of finance, which is more complicated than you ever realized.

Wherever you turn for financial advice, I strongly encourage you to always prioritize feelings of peace and comfort with your advisor. You should never, ever fear the individual(s) you choose to oversee your finances. In fact, a good advisor puts you at complete and total ease about your financial future while still being honest about your situation. At the same time, don't let freshly baked cookies and warm fuzzies cloud your judgment. Your advisor may be the friendliest person you know, but if they're not doing a good job it might be time to look elsewhere.

Recently, a co-worker sent me a satirical piece on 401(k) management in the U.S., prompting a conversation about what makes a good advisor. We found ourselves talking about what characteristics we would look for if we were personally in the market for a financial advisor, which led to the following list.

We Would Want an Advisor Who
Is a Fiduciary

Different types of investment professionals are held to different standards by various government regulatory agencies. My colleague and I decided one of our top priorities would be to hire an advisor who is held to a *fiduciary standard*.

A fiduciary is legally obligated to put your best interests first. Other professionals are held only to a *suitability standard*, which requires them to provide you with "good enough" options, not the best option. This standard is crucial because you want someone who is looking out for your very best interests, not simply offering "appropriate" advice.

Has Good Credentials

My co-worker and I agreed that we would look for an advisor who had credentials above and beyond the base regulatory requirements established by relevant government agencies (known as licenses). In our opinion, the licensing requirements for becoming an advisor aren't difficult to satisfy.

That's why we would look for an advisor who had demonstrated expertise in the field by obtaining well-respected credentials such as the CFP® (certified financial planner), CPA (certified public accountant), or CFA® (chartered financial analyst) designations. See Appendix B for more about the various designations and certifications for advisors.

Values Continuing Education

In addition to the credentials in the previous section, we would look for an advisor who continued to pursue education so he or she could remain an expert. Because the laws regarding taxes and financial planning constantly change, we believe a commitment to continuing education demonstrates that an advisor is constantly learning and seeking to stay relevant for the sake of his or her clients.

Offers Competitive Fees

Searching for an advisor is akin to other big financial decisions where quality matters, such as upgrading the windows in your house or installing a home theater. You don't want to overpay, but you also don't want to underpay and end up with something cheap that doesn't perform well.

Fees detract from your bottom line, but an advisor who asks for very little may be doing very little, which could also hurt your bottom line. Do your research so that you know what financial advisors typically charge in your area. Firms typically set their fees to be competitive with other nearby firms, which is one way you can get a good idea about what you should expect to pay. When you interview advisors, ask them what they'll be doing to earn their fee and once you've hired one, follow up periodically to make sure they continue providing all the services they said they would.

Is Honest and Transparent

When my husband and I closed on our first home, our loan officer was incredibly open and honest about each and every detail of the transaction. His transparency and commitment to answering our questions made the experience so much easier than I had anticipated.

In a world filled with fraud and scandal, I believe that honesty and transparency are incredibly valuable traits in a financial professional. I highly regard any advisor who can provide me with a feeling of safety and security and who has a track record of doing ethical business, and I recommend that you look for an advisor who can do the same for you.

What's in a Statement

While your advisor is legally required to provide you with periodic financial statements on your accounts, it can sometimes be difficult to decipher those statements. Here are a couple of things to look for when reading your statements.

Returns

It may surprise you to find that there is more than one way to calculate the performance of your account. In my opinion, the easiest calculation is what is known as the "holding period return," which is basically your ending balance divided by your beginning balance minus one. For example, if I started with $100 and ended with $105, my holding period return would be 5 percent (105/100 − 1 = .05). Unfortunately, investing is rarely that simple, which is why so many other formulas exist for calculating returns. While we won't go into the more complex math, here are two of the more popular return calculations that you may find on your statements.

- *Time-weighted return (TWR):* This return calculation focuses on the timing of your investments (when the different investments are made), making it a little bit more accurate than a simple holding period return calculation.
- *Internal rate of return (IRR):* This return has to do with

the movement of cash into and out of the account and the growth rate that causes the outflows to equal the inflows. It is sometimes also called the money-weighted return (MWR). There are limitations to the calculation for the IRR, particularly when negative performance is present, which is why it's usually best to use the TWR calculation for presenting performance.

Gross vs. Net

Another set of terms you may hear when it comes to performance reporting is gross versus net. You can think of the *gross return* as the return on your investments before all of the fees have been deducted and *net return* as the return on your investments after all of the fees have been deducted. For example, let's say that your gross annual return was 5 percent, but your investment advisor charges you 1 percent. That would mean that your net annual return is actually 4 percent (5 − 1 = 4). The net number is more important than the gross number because it is the actual total return to you after all of your expenses on investing. One of the best ways to tell if your advisor is being transparent about performance and fees is whether they show net performance.

Standardized Time Periods

One of the best ways to identify good financial reporting is consistency. When you receive your statements, compare them to prior statements and see if they are formatted similarly, particularly when it comes to time periods. Industry best practice dictates using a set of common time periods for performance reporting on every statement. These time periods should include year-to-date and previous (or rolling) 12 months as a minimum. Some advisors may also choose to include other time periods such as previous 3 months, quarter to date, or previous 6 months. What's important is that your advisor provides the same metrics in each report. If the time ranges look weird or the metrics are constantly changing, it may mean that your advisor is cherry picking performance and only showing you the numbers that can be viewed positively.

Benchmarks

While advisors aren't required to include a benchmark, it can be an incredibly helpful tool to help you understand your performance. Similar to time periods, you'll want to look for consistency. If your advisor is comparing your performance to a different benchmark each time, then the benchmarks do you no good. A good benchmark is one that you can understand and that makes sense for your investments. A benchmark related exclusively to stock performance tells you very little about how your bond-heavy investments are performing. Similarly, if you don't know what's in a benchmark or don't understand the name, there's no way of knowing if you're comparing apples to apples or apples to kumquats. If you don't understand a benchmark, ask your advisor to clarify.

Reading Disclaimers

Finally, while disclaimers can be dry, boring, and hard to read, it's important not to ignore them—especially when it comes to financial reporting. On multiple occasions, I have found myself marveling at a fund's performance only to read in the disclaimer that the performance is hypothetical or based on back-testing and not what actually happened. Disclaimers exist because they are meant to hold advisors accountable for the data they're providing to you, but the only way that works is if you take the time to read and understand the disclaimers.

Learn More

These are just a few things to consider when it comes to investment reporting. If you would like to learn more about how performance calculations work, how to read your statements, or what certain terms mean, start with the following third-party resources.

- *North American Securities Administrators Association:* Understanding Your Brokerage Account Statements (http://www.nasaa.org/wp-content/uploads/2011/08/ SIFMA-SIPC-NASAA-Broker-Statements-Brochure.pdf)
- *U.S. Securities and Exchange Commission:* Information for the Individual Investor (http://www.sec.gov/investor)

Spotting a Scam

Whenever I think of financial scams, I think of the "President's Fund." I first heard of this "secret fund" when an individual emailed me to ask if I thought it was a good idea. The fund was advertised as a "top secret" investment that had previously only been available to U.S. presidents and promised outstanding returns, but—whaddya know—for a short period of time it was being offered to this individual for a special introductory price. Red flags went up everywhere. This thing was clearly not what it claimed to be. I spent an afternoon poking around the internet to see what others had to say about the President's Fund, and it didn't take me long to discover that the fund was actually just an annuity and a really crummy one at that.

The scary thing is, some scams can appear to be totally legit. And some totally legit investments will almost certainly never make you any money. These types of deals usually include investments in things like real estate, private equity, and start-up firms, which are known in the financial world as alternative investments because they are alternatives to traditional stocks and bonds that are publicly traded on a regulated exchange. While some may actually be good opportunities, the alternative space is full of horrible deals and outright scams.

To help you keep your guard up, let's look at some situations you might encounter and the most important things to remember in each of those situations.

Situation

A financial salesperson approaches you with "a great deal you can't find anywhere else."

Things to Consider

Always be skeptical of special deals. If this deal is so great, why is the salesperson sharing it instead of keeping it for himself? If someone approached me and said this is the best car I've ever had—it works perfectly, it has great gas mileage, but I'd be happy to sell it to you—I would be pretty confused. If it's so great, why doesn't she want it? Remember, if someone is selling you something, they are expecting to make money too. Don't be afraid to ask a salesperson how they will make money on the deal and why they're offering it in the first place. You want their interests to be aligned with yours.

Red Flags

- The deal is difficult to understand.
- The return numbers are incredibly high.

Situation

Your financial advisor sends you an advertisement for an exclusive, limited-time-only, real estate deal.

Things to Consider

In this day and age, real estate deals are plentiful, but few are actually done well, particularly because there are so many unknowns. Whenever you're considering a real estate deal, it's important to really dig into the underlying research. Most shady financial salespeople are expecting their prospective clients to be at least a little confused. Don't give them that benefit. There is no shame in asking a lot of questions, and there is great value in recognizing your limitations. If you know you're not an expert on real estate, get a second opinion from someone who is before entering into a binding contract that could lock up your capital for a long time.

Red Flags

- There are a lot of pictures, but no numbers backing up the investment.
- The ownership structure is complex and vague.
- There is no mention of potential risks or the amount of debt that will be used.
- There is a long lock-up period.

Situation

A financial advisor offers to invest you in an up and coming start-up, claiming that the growth opportunities are endless.

Things to Consider

A good rule of thumb whenever you encounter a special deal is to recognize that if something sounds too good to be true, it probably is. While there are historical instances of investments that have had incredibly high returns, they are overshadowed by promises of incredible opportunities that have blown up and caused a lot of pain for investors.

Start-ups have to offer high returns because they are incredibly risky and have a high probability of failing. If you are considering investing in a start-up because it's something you believe in, one of the best ways to protect yourself is to not invest more than you can handle losing. In other words, don't bet the farm. Ask yourself: if this investment doesn't work out and I lose everything I invest, will I be OK?

Red Flags

- The advisor offering the deal is connected to the start-up in some way, shape, or form and stands to benefit from you investing. This is called a conflict of interest and should be clearly disclosed by the advisor.
- The start-up is looking to raise 100 percent of its capital. If the company management itself has no skin in the game, it also has little incentive to succeed.
- You Google the start-up and can't find a physical address or location.
- The start-up hasn't started yet.

Learn More

If you'd like to learn more about how to defend yourself against financial schemes go to www.letsmakeaplan.org and check out their guides on financial self-defense.

PART 3

Getting Started:
The Basics

I hope you find true meaning, contentment,
and passion in your life. I hope you navigate the difficult
times and come out with greater strength and resolve.
I hope you find whatever balance you seek with
your eyes wide open.

—Sheryl Sandberg, 2011 Barnard College
Commencement Address

Over the course of my education I have taken dozens of classes. I have taken classes in economics, international relations, religion, the humanities, finance, and even music theory. Not once did I take a class on how to budget my money, save for retirement, or choose my health benefits—things that would have been enormously helpful to know when I started my career. This section is about the basics of *personal* finance—the things you need to know to set you on the right path for financial success.

In Part 2, I tried to show you around the financial kitchen and point out some major tools and give you some ideas about how to use them. In Part 3, we are going to pull out some recipes you can use to cook up a productive life. All these recipes can be modified to best fit your personal tastes and family situations, of course, but I hope you will find the concepts helpful in many situations.

To start off, we'll talk about negotiating your salary and maximizing your benefits at work. Then I'll walk you through a sample budget and give you some tips for paying off debt in addition to explaining credit scores and reports. Finally, we'll talk about how debt can be used as a force for good and what it looks like to plan an awesome wedding on a budget. Once you've finished Part 3, you should have a good idea of how to live within your means and to spend and save with an eye towards the future.

CHAPTER 6

Suits and Lattes

WHEN I WAS A TEENAGER, I was convinced that I wasn't the marrying, child-rearing type. What I desperately wanted was to get out of the suburbs where I grew up and *be* somebody. I was going to be a "working woman" who wore stylish suits—the tailored kind that tell everyone that you're a woman who's going places. I was going to live in New York City, ride around in shiny yellow cabs, carry piping hot lattes, and talk on the phone all the time.

But shortly after I graduated college, I found myself married to a sweet boy with a scruffy beard who wanted to move back to my hometown of Arvada, Colorado, to learn about extractive metallurgy. (To this day, I am still not entirely sure what extractive metallurgy is, but people say it's a thing.) So here I am. Back in the suburbs where I grew up, married, and a mommy. I make my own coffee, and my day-to-day uniform consists of leggings and comfy sweaters. Life is funny that way.

My first job after college was a bit of a disappointment. I think most first jobs are. In hindsight, however, I think I owe a lot of who I am and how far I've come professionally to that first job. I was passionate and idealistic when I first graduated from college. I'm still passionate, but I've come down from the clouds a bit, and I'd like to think I have a much more realistic view of the working world, in part because that first job turned out to be a bit of a refining process. You can learn a surprising amount when you have no other choice.

There were a lot of things I didn't like about that job, but I had no ability to change any of the circumstances that were making me so unhappy. As my workload became heavier and heavier, I became angry and bitter. I often cried on my drive home. I fussed with my husband. That job was slowly stamping out the life-force in my soul, so I did what I had to. I quit, ate a bunch of pizza and cupcakes, and slowly healed. Then I refreshed my résumé and found a new job working for a company whose mission aligned with my own. That turned out to be one of the best decisions I have ever made.

Finding Purpose and Value

I believe that the work you do has a huge effect on your attitude toward life. Purpose matters. When you believe that your work has purpose, it becomes valuable to you; and when you believe your work is valuable, then you begin to believe that you are valuable. As it turns out, I'm just as valuable to my employer working in my leggings from my suburban home office as I would be as a suit-wearing, latte-carrying executive in a high-rise office in New York City. And the lessons I learned in my first difficult job have helped me understand that my value is not linked to my company or position or office attire, and I will be forever grateful for the chance to learn that lesson so early.

Whether you're starting a new career fresh out of school or are returning to the workforce after taking time off to raise a gaggle of kids, I hope you know that you have the power to incite change and make a difference, even if that difference is primarily in your local sphere of influence. We live in a time and society that offers unprecedented opportunities for women, and many aspects of our culture not only accept our participation but actually encourage us to shake things up. More than ever before, women are becoming engineers, doctors, and CEOs. The world needs your passion and enthusiasm, whether you are leading a Fortune 500 company, running a one-woman design firm from home, or working as an administrative assistant in a local accountant's office.

Of course, this wide-open world of choices can sometimes lead to nagging anxieties when we wonder if we are living up to our full potential or accomplishing as much as our peers. Whether you are in an entry-level position or in the top management ranks, you most likely still have days when you doubt that you are on the "right track." If you feel a little lost, then you're probably part of the majority. You just don't know that because most of us are too chicken to admit that's how we feel. When you go out for drinks with your peers, you're supposed to talk about how quickly you're achieving your life goals, or how many places you've traveled, or how spacious your renovated, uptown, classy gal apartment is. Personally, I've grown tired of that conversation because it feels inauthentic.

I want to know who you are more than I want to know what you've done. Your achievements are just icing on the cupcake. If you don't like your job and you feel like being an adult is messy and hard and you're not sure you're on the right trajectory, rest assured that you're OK. I feel that way too, sometimes. Most of us do.

On the other hand, if you're crushing it and loving it, I want to genuinely congratulate you. I hope you have the grace to encourage others who don't feel they are quite there yet.

Wherever you are on whatever track you have chosen, I hope you continue to pursue your dreams because passionate people make the world a better place. In the meantime, you will also need to make decisions about salaries, benefits, and retirement plans. Even dreamers need health insurance. Whether you are in your first job out of college or in your third decade with the same company, your decisions in these areas can have a tremendous effect on your feelings of purpose and value and even color your opinions of your employer or career choices. So let's consider how you should approach these decisions—especially if you are facing them for the first time.

Negotiating Your Salary

I started my first job the month after I graduated college. It was a time of major transition as I began to realize how little my studies had prepared me for the logistics of being an adult. From figuring out what type of health insurance was best to understanding the terms of a lease, I felt completely overwhelmed. I was so caught up in the excitement of simply having a job that I completely overlooked the opportunity to negotiate my salary. The guy who hired me said, "How about this much?" I said, "Sure." And that was that. It turns out that I did what most women tend to do. Negotiating future salary should be part of starting any new job, but we women have, historically, been bad at it.

This problem is examined in a 2007 book, *Women Don't Ask* by Linda Babcock, a professor of economics at Carnegie

Mellon, and Sara Laschever, a lecturer on the challenges women face in the modern workforce. In the introduction, Babcock tells a story from her time serving as the director of the PhD program at her university.

Many of the male graduate students were teaching courses of their own, the women explained, while most of the female graduate students had been assigned to work as teaching assistants to regular faculty. Linda agreed that this didn't sound fair, and that afternoon she asked the associate dean who handled teaching assignments about the women's complaint. She received a simple answer: "I try to find teaching opportunities for any student who approaches me with a good idea for a course, the ability to teach, and a reasonable offer about what it will cost," he explained. "More men ask. The women just don't ask." [12]

Writing as a woman in finance, I know what it means to be in the minority. As I mentioned in the "Introduction," in the financial planning industry only 26 percent of advisors are women.[13] When it comes to the actual investing portion of the finance world, only 16.4 percent of the roughly 51,000 active CFA® members (a well-known institution in the world of finance) are women.[14] Historically, women have been the underdogs in the workforce, but that is *historically.* Today, more women are entering the workforce than ever before. In 1970, only 38 percent of the female population were in jobs in the labor force, but 57 percent were there in 2014. Despite that increase in numbers, the median weekly income of women in 2014 was $719 compared to $871 for men.[15] Many factors affect that discrepancy, but I believe one major reason that women make less than men may be that we're simply not asking for more money.

Avoid "Just-ifying" Requests

In May 2015, former Google and Apple exec Ellen Petry Leanse wrote an article titled "'Just' Say No" that quickly went viral. In the article, she discusses how often women use the word "just" and the connotations that come with it: "It hit me that there was something about the word I didn't like. It was a 'permission' word, in a way—a warm-up to a request, an apology for interrupting, a shy knock on a door before asking 'Can I get something I need from you?'"[16]

The more Leanse heard women use the word, the more she became convinced that it implied subordination and that she needed to remove it from her vocabulary. As she did, she and her female colleagues who took similar actions began noticing a significant change in their self-confidence. Something as simple as the words we use to communicate with others could be key to understanding how women negotiate their salary and why they earn less.

Recognize Your Value

The first step to negotiating a good salary is to believe that you are worth one. As I mentioned earlier, in the financial world we see that value is tied to price, and this is true when it comes to compensation as well. You don't need to ask for permission to be valuable. If you got the job offer, then they see something in you, and you should be proud of that. Of course, you probably shouldn't walk into a negotiating room and immediately ask a potential employer to double an initial offer. You want to be confident *and* reasonable.

When it comes to the logistics of negotiating your salary, you need to be armed with good data about typical wages for your position and your location. A good starting place to compile such data is the almighty internet. Websites like

Glassdoor and Indeed have a decent amount of data on salaries for different jobs. I also suggest checking out wage-project.org. WAGE stands for Women Are Getting Even. Not only does the site provide median wage numbers for hundreds of different job titles at different experience and education levels, but it also offers additional information on benefits and what type of total compensation you should expect to receive for your given area of work.

Use Facts Wisely
Spend some time on these sites learning about the salaries of individuals with positions and work experience similar to your own. Develop a range of pay that feels appropriate to you and be ready to justify your request to your new employer. Keep in mind that most employers are results-oriented. Consider agreeing to a lower starting wage if the employer will promise additional compensation tied to specific goals you hope to achieve. This puts you on the same side of the table as the employer because when the company grows as a result of your hard work, you both do well.

Finally, make sure that your body language matches your words. Stand up straight and look the negotiator in the eye. Don't say "just" or apologize for your wage requests. Confidence is key. And remember, it never hurts to ask.

Picking Your Health-Care Benefits
Choosing health insurance is one of the most confusing things you will ever do. I believe this with my whole heart. Before I try to explain a bunch of completely unhelpful acronyms and cryptic words, I think it's helpful to spend some time considering why this decision is so important

and why you should do your research before enrolling. Health care has the potential to become very expensive very quickly. You can be as healthy as a horse but suddenly need an emergency appendectomy. Who is going to pay for that? Health insurance and/or you. The type of health insurance you sign up for determines whether you or the insurance company will pay the bulk of such unexpected bills.

It's also important to remember that health *insurance* is just that—another form of insurance. You are insuring against an event. Similar to other types of insurance, in some instances it is worth it to pay a portion out of your pocket for health-care services. Consider how healthy you are when choosing your health insurance plan. If you exercise regularly, eat healthy, and don't get sick often, it doesn't make sense for you to sign up for the most expensive health insurance plan. Of course, just because you're healthy today doesn't mean that you won't need health care tomorrow, so it doesn't make sense for you to skimp on coverage for unexpected events, either. You want to find a balance. With that in mind, let's dig in.

HMO

Typically, when you sign up for health insurance you have the opportunity to choose between an HMO and a PPO, which is why I'll address those acronyms first. HMO stands for health maintenance organization; in an HMO, you can use only the doctors, medical providers, and hospitals that are part of the organization providing the insurance.[17] Think of HMOs as all-you-can-eat buffets. You can load up your plate with everything you need: annual checkups, dermatology, gynecology, obstetrics, etc., all at the same place. You can't, however, go to the restaurant next door even if it has your favorite dessert because your insurance only covers the buffet at the first restaurant.

Your healthcare is simplified with an HMO, because all services are provided through the same organization, which means less paperwork and fewer administrative rules that you need to figure out and keep track of. I chose to enroll in an HMO because I had grown up with one and was familiar with how they worked. In hindsight, this turned out to be a great decision when I needed surgery and again when I decided to have a baby. I had my initial examinations, ultrasound procedures, and surgery through the same organization. When I became pregnant, all of my appointments and the delivery went through the same organization. I didn't have to find a different provider for each additional step along the way, and my out-of-pocket costs were all based on one rate schedule. I never had to pay a fee and then file paperwork to ask the insurance company for reimbursement for what I had paid. This simplicity made potentially scary times significantly less stressful.

However, know that HMO plans have drawbacks— mainly that you don't get to shop around for your doctors and other health-care providers. If you are very picky about your health care and like to check out different doctors or medical offices, an HMO plan may not be your best choice because it offers less flexibility about which providers you can use. If you choose to visit a doctor or medical services provider who is not part of your HMO, you will likely end up paying a large portion of the full cost of your care. There are exceptions for emergency situations, however. What those exceptions are and how they work are plan specific.

PPO

A PPO is a preferred provider organization. If an HMO is like a restaurant buffet plan, a PPO plan is more like a rewards card that works in a whole slew of restaurants.[18] If you choose a PPO plan, you will be given a list of doctors, hospitals, and other health care providers that are in the PPO "network." As long as you use these in-network providers, you will pay smaller out-of-pocket fees for your health care. Think of the PPO "network" as an approved list of restaurants where you can get discounts on your meals with your rewards card. At one of my previous employers, my vision and dental plans were structured in the form of a PPO, which meant that I would go to the PPO's website to find a list of in-network dentists or optometrists in my area. If they were part of the network, my insurance would pay for most of the cost of the visit or procedure. Some PPO plans will also allow you to use providers not on their network list, but you will usually pay a higher fee for any care.

A PPO provides you with significantly more flexibility regarding your doctors and medical providers, which is a real plus if you like to shop around for your medical care. A PPO plan typically also offers more location options than an HMO does, which may be helpful if you want to choose a doctor close to your home.

The downside of using a PPO is that each office you visit will likely be different, with its own unique policies and procedures for processing your out-of-pocket payments and working with your insurance company. This variability frustrated me when I was looking for an optometrist because I could never completely tell what my PPO insurance covered in a particular office. It seemed I was always getting charged additional fees that were not covered by the insurance plan.

Should you choose the PPO option, I would highly encourage you to call any potential medical offices prior to making an appointment. Ask them to explain exactly how their billing works and what your insurance covers. That way, you won't find any surprises when you show up for your visit or get your bill. Another drawback to PPO plans is that you may be required to go to multiple doctors and provider offices if you find yourself in need of specialty care.

Deductible

Both deductibles and co-pays are considered types of "cost-sharing," meaning they're both a type of fee that you must pay out of your pocket. Think of a deductible as the maximum amount you must pay each year before your insurance company will step in and start paying its fair share for your medical costs.

Let's say you have a deductible of $2,000. This means that you must pay at least $2,000 for your own health-care procedures before your insurance company will kick in and start covering its share of the costs for the rest of that year. I think this article, written by a nurse, from the Verywell website does an excellent job of laying out how this works:

You have a $2,000 deductible. You get the flu in January and see your doctor. The doctor's bill is $200. You are responsible for the entire bill since you haven't paid your deductible yet this year. After paying the $200 doctor's bill, you have $1,800 left to go on your yearly deductible.

In March, you fall and break your arm. The bill is $3,000. You pay $1,800 of that bill before you've met your yearly deductible of $2,000. Now, your health insurance kicks in and helps you pay the rest of the bill.

In April, you get your cast removed. The bill is $500. Since you've already met your deductible for the year, you don't have to pay any more toward your deductible. Your health insurance pays its full share of this bill.[19]

As you can see from the example, a deductible is a fixed maximum amount that you pay each year. Usually, the higher your deductible is, the less your insurance will cost because you are offering to pay a larger share of your own medical bills. This may benefit you if you are healthy and unlikely to have a lot of medical expenses. If you usually only go to the doctor once or twice each year, then it makes sense for you to simply pay the cost of those visits out of pocket, which will mean that you pay less for your health insurance.

Remember, insurance is largely there to insure you against unexpected catastrophic events. If you have to pay a deductible, you may ask yourself why you should even bother purchasing insurance if you're still required to pay additional out-of-pocket costs. But consider the fact that an unanticipated surgery may cost tens of thousands of dollars. At that point, having to pay only $2,000 before your insurance company starts covering a share of the rest of the bills starts to sound like a pretty good deal.

Co-pay

A co-pay is similar to a deductible in that it is a portion of your medical expenses that you are required to pay. Unlike the annual nature of the deductible, however, a co-pay is a fixed sum that you pay each time you receive certain medical services. For example, a health-care plan could require a co-pay of $15 each time you visit the doctor, $50 each time you go to the emergency room, and $100 for some other medical procedures. Some co-pays are determined in the form of percentages, such as 10 or 20 percent of the total cost of the medical visit or procedure.

Some health insurance plans have a deductible *and* a co-pay, which means you must cover your annual deductible each year and then make your co-pay for medical services after the deductible is met. Others are either/or—you have either a deductible or a co-pay system. It's important to consider the tradeoffs between deductibles, co-pays, and insurance premiums when you sign up for coverage. Pay attention to your current state of health and think about how often you visit the doctor each year.

Premiums

Your health insurance premiums are the amount that must be paid by you and/or your employer for your health insurance coverage. They can be paid on a monthly, quarterly, or annual basis depending on how the plan is set up. How much you pay in premiums depends on several factors, including how old you are, where you live, whether or not you smoke, if the insurance is just for you or for your whole family, and the type of plan you choose.[20] The younger you are, the cheaper your plan will be because the health insurance number gurus are assuming you're healthier and less likely to find yourself in a catastrophic situation that requires the insurance company to fork over a ton of money to pay for medical procedures to help make you well. Where you live, the population of your area, and the local cost of living will also impact your premiums. Of course, if you are insuring a family of four instead of just one, the plan will cost more.

Finally, the type of plan you choose will likely determine

how large your deductible or co-pays will be. As I mentioned previously, the more you pay out of pocket in the form of a higher deductible, the lower your premiums are likely to be. The highest-ranked health insurance plans (think platinum, diamond, or some other fancy term) have the highest premiums and the lowest out-of-pocket costs—meaning you will pay more in premiums, but the insurance company will pay more of your actual medical bills. Think of it as just another trade-off. If you don't think you'll spend a lot of time at the doctor, go for the higher deductible. You likely won't max it out but you will save on the lower premiums.

FSA

FSA stands for Flexible Spending Account and is one of the more common health insurance benefits offered by employers to their employees. An FSA allows you to stash cash for medical expenses in a tax-friendly manner. FSAs do not have eligibility requirements, but there are limits to how much you can contribute to an account. You'll want to check the IRS website each year to stay up to date on the frequently changing annual limit. Contributions must be made with pretax money, and withdrawals from the account are not taxed. FSA money must be used for qualified medical expenses and has to be used by the end of the year—which is why you'll hear it described as a "use it or lose it" account.

HSA

HSA stands for Health Savings Account, which is only available to individuals with a high deductible health insurance plan. FSA and HSA accounts are either/or—you can't have both even if your employer offers both. Contributions for this type of account are also capped, but the limit is higher for HSAs than for FSAs. HSA balances also roll over each year, so individuals with an HSA can use their account well into retirement for qualified medical expenses. Contributions are also tax-deductible, grow tax-free, and remain tax-free once distributed. You can learn more about both types of accounts at HealthCare.gov.

Company Retirement Plans

When you're just starting out in your career, retirement may seem like something in the very distant future. In reality, the choices you make early on play a big role in determining how well prepared you will be for retirement when the time finally does come.

One of the worst approaches you can take is to put it off "until later." Often, I hear young women respond to a question about saving for retirement with some version of: "I'll worry about that down the road." It's an easy answer but also an unwise one for many. The truth is, saving is a habit that you develop over time, and developing savings habits later in life can be very difficult.

That's why I highly encourage younger clients to get in the habit of saving what they can now, even if it feels inconsequential. Set aside $50 a month. The next time you get a raise, up the amount to $100 a month. Keep pushing yourself to increase your monthly savings until you're able to max out what you're putting away for retirement. Retiring costs a lot (as you will see later in the book). For now, suffice it to say you should be stashing away a decent amount if you hope to retire at a reasonable age.

If you can't stash a lot away right now, that's OK—as long as you are building a habit of saving and setting yourself up to save more in the future in a manner that will actually force you to do it. When it comes to *how* you should save, you'll need to know about different types of retirement plans.

Pension

A pension is a type of retirement benefit classified as a "defined benefit." This is because your employer defines the benefit you will receive when you retire. Pensions are usually based on a complex calculation of your age, how long you've worked at a company, and how long an actuary thinks you're going to live. Most pensions either pay out in a large lump sum when you retire or in monthly installments until you die.

Although pensions are super awesome for employees, they're also very expensive to maintain for employers. Those employers would rather pass the burden of your retirement onto you, which is why pensions have become increasingly rare and also why this paragraph is pretty short. (If you have a pension and need some help understanding how it works you can find my contact info at the end of this book.)

401(k)

A 401(k) is a type of retirement account classified as "defined contribution." It's called this because you define what you will contribute. If you work at a nonprofit, the equivalent option is called a 403(b), and if you work for a government entity you're probably going to be offered a 457. Both function like a 401(k). When it comes to 401(k) s, the burden of saving for retirement is on you. Luckily, most employers incentivize your savings through something magical called matching.

Matching

Many employers offer to match at least part of their employees' contributions to their retirement plans, such as 401(k) accounts. Here's a pretty solid financial planning rule of thumb you should always remember: if your employer matches your contributions to your retirement funds, you should contribute. Why? Because those matches are free money. As in FREE MONEY.

Even if you can't handle maxing out your 401(k), do yourself a favor and contribute at least as much as your employer is willing to match. You don't have to work extra for those matching funds. Saying no to the match is like saying no if your employer offers to hand you a couple extra thousand dollars a year to leave work on time.

In finance-speak, matching usually looks something like this: your employer will match 100 percent of your contributions up to x percent (usually somewhere between 3 percent and 6 percent). This means if you contribute one percent of your paycheck to your 401(k), your employer will match that contribution dollar for dollar. If one percent of your paycheck equals $200, you will be adding $200 to your 401(k) and your employer will add *another* $200 to your 401(k) (also known as FREE MONEY). You should contribute enough to get the full match. End of story.

Traditional or Roth

When you have the option of contributing to a 401(k) at work, you may also have the option of deciding how you will contribute. This usually consists of two choices: pre-tax contributions and post-tax contributions—also known as Roth contributions. A traditional 401(k) is structured so that you receive tax deductions for your contributions. Your money grows tax deferred—meaning you don't have to pay taxes on changes in the account value in the interim. You will, however, have to pay taxes when you pull the money out for retirement.

Conversely, a 401(k) funded with post-tax money means you pay taxes on the money that you put into the fund, but that money will grow tax-free essentially forever. To help you decide whether to choose traditional or Roth, we at Cedarstone have created what we call the "Traditional vs. Roth Contributions Game Plan," which I will lay out for you here. This game plan also applies to IRAs.

Traditional vs. Roth Contributions Game Plan

In Your Twenties

In your earliest working years, begin saving for retirement in a Roth 401(k). In these years you are likely making less than you will later in your career, thereby placing you in a lower tax bracket. Furthermore, you have many years until retirement. By saving in a Roth early on you get to take full advantage of the tax-free growth that follows.

In Your Thirties

As you earn more, you will slowly be moving into higher tax brackets, but your earnings may be offset by deductions for a mortgage or dependents if you choose to buy a house or have children. Still, it is a good idea to target Roth contributions first if it is possible for you to live without the immediate tax deduction.

In Your Forties

Most individuals begin to hit peak earning years during this time, but it is usually still best to contribute to a Roth 401(k). Admittedly the benefit of the Roth account is less than it was a couple of decades earlier since you are likely in a higher tax bracket and are closer to needing the money; however, in the long run, having assets that aren't taxable can be a huge benefit once you're retired. If you are in a higher tax bracket, you may want to consider splitting your contribution so you can get both the tax benefit of deducting traditional contributions and the benefit of having tax-free money later on. Consider discussing your situation with a financial planner. Making the right decision could save you thousands in taxes over time.

In Your Fifties

At this point, you are beginning to approach retirement and likely should be contributing to a traditional 401(k). Once you reach the age of fifty you also become eligible for what the IRS refers to as "catch up contributions," which are intended to help individuals "catch up" on their retirement savings by allowing them to contribute extra money each year to their retirement accounts (there is a limit to how much you can contribute).

In Your Sixties

Once you reach retirement, depending on your situation, you may want to convert some of your traditional 401(k) money into a Roth IRA. In doing so, you will need to pay the relevant taxes, but after the conversion the Roth money will grow tax-free. This option is not right for everyone, so consult with your financial planner about your specific situation. This is a good option to consider especially if you have a large 401(k) or IRA that you will not spend during your lifetime. Roth money is much better to leave to heirs and is not subject to required minimum distributions,* which require you to take certain sums from your accounts after you reach age 70.5 (more on that later), making Roth accounts a very helpful tool later in life.

*While not subject to RMDs during your lifetime, an inherited Roth account will be subject to RMDs for your heirs.

CHAPTER 7

I Hate Exercise (but Still Run)! Debt and Budgeting

WHEN I WAS SIX, my parents signed me up for T-ball in an attempt to gauge my athletic prowess. I saw T-ball as an opportunity to chat with my friend and engage with the ball and everyone else on a minimal basis. Thus began my preference for solitary activities that involve sitting down. By the time I started high school I was really good at not being athletic, which was unfortunate since my high school served pizza and Chik-fil-A on a regular basis. Consequently, my habit of doing nothing combined with crappy cafeteria food led to an unfortunate amount of what I like to describe as *fluffiness* during my teenage years. To combat said fluffiness I took up "slow" running.

I hate running. I am not one of those girls at the gym with the cute outfits and the perfect ponytail who prances along on the treadmill like a glittery unicorn. I am an ugly runner. I have short hair that won't fit into a ponytail but instead flares out around my headband—giving me the appearance of a sweaty lion. I have short, stumpy legs and when I run it looks more like I'm scurrying. My nose runs incessantly while I'm running, so I spend the majority of the time wiping it on my clothing. It's a real turn-on. I'm a pathetic runner, but I run because at a very low point during my teenage-hood I realized that I had to start taking care of myself. Otherwise, I would continue to add "fluff," and my body deserved better than that from me.

In 2016 I ran my first half-marathon. It took me a little over three hours; a couple who walked half of it finished ahead of me. Nevertheless, crossing that finish line was one of the proudest moments of my life to date. I signed up for the race because I wanted to prove to myself that I had the discipline and endurance to finish. I love the word *endure*. There's something powerful about being able to look back on the things you have endured in your lifetime and embrace the strength that comes from knowing you survived. I distinctly remember reaching mile seven of the half-marathon. I had just passed my family, who were cheering from inside their car on the side of the road, and thought I had crested the last remaining hill only to look up and see a significantly higher hill in front of me. Up until this point, I had felt pretty good about the run. Seven miles was a typical distance for me, and I was still trotting along at a decent pace, but the sight of that hill made my heart sink. Still, I was determined not to fall behind some of the speed walkers, so I put my head down, turned up my iPod, and leaned into it. Making it to the top of that next hill was my favorite part of the whole race because I knew I had conquered the hardest part. Everything else was downhill.

We all have hills in our lives—impossible-looking obstacles that threaten to crush us. When it comes to finances, debt can often feel like a hill that can't be conquered. How can we begin to save when we don't know how to start paying off the debt that's accumulated? When staring at that scary-looking hill, it's important to remember that the debt probably didn't show up overnight, and it won't be conquered all at once either. Instead, we have to attack it the same way I attacked that hill at mile seven: one step at a time. Bit by bit, you will make progress on your debt mountain until suddenly you crest the top and catch your first glimpse of the breathtaking view known as financial freedom.

The fastest way to get on top of your debt is through careful budgeting. Budgeting is hard because it may require us to face some major demons that have gained power over us by our own poor choices, such as credit card debt or bad spending habits. The first step is the hardest and also the most important: just start. Sit down with a pen and paper or open an Excel spreadsheet on your laptop and start investigating where your money goes. One of my favorite websites for budgeting is mint.com. Mint allows you to link all of your accounts together in one place and then import and track your spending so you can easily see where your money is being spent. Once you've done this, you can begin building a budget for how your money *should be* spent. Slowly, step-by-step, you can make your way up the hill to financial stability.

Why You Need a Budget
(and How to Build One)

Creating and following a budget is the secret to taking back your financial freedom and getting your spending under control. I know "budget" is a lame word that boring people in ill-fitting suits use a lot, but it's one of those things that keeps you out of trouble—like paying your taxes and drinking your morning coffee. You won't magically start spending less just because you listen to a man named "Mikey the

Money Magician" on the radio. You will spend less when you stop buying as much. This process requires self-discipline, which is a very valuable character trait that few of us have (including me, especially when it comes to cookies).

If you need to take a course on financial peace or money management, go for it! I know a lot of friends who have used Dave Ramsey's *Financial Peace University* and had a very positive experience. Please do not feel judged or condemned if you need to ask for help. If you are in an ugly place with massive levels of debt, getting help from a professional may be the best option for you. If you are facing more manageable levels of debt or just looking to save more money, check out these helpful budgeting tips that work for my family and may work for yours.

Coupons

Coupons are real, and I love them. Because this is the twenty-first century, you can find coupons simply by Googling "coupons for (insert item here)." A Target app called Cartwheel lets you scan barcodes on different items and then download any coupons for that item that might be out there in the universe somewhere. It's amazing! Other major chains have similar apps with similar coupons and deals that you can pull up on your smartphone while shopping. I personally have apps for my local grocery store and several of my favorite home décor stores on my phone that I pull up whenever I'm out running errands.

Food for Thought

Using coupons will help you spend less only if you don't use your savings as an excuse to buy more! For example: a coupon that helps you save 10 percent on laundry detergent does not give you leeway to buy a second jug of laundry detergent or twelve bottles of nail polish. If you do that, you may wind up spending more even if you're saving more. Use your coupons to cut down on your receipt total—not as an excuse to add additional items.

Food and Drink

Food and drink are expensive and often a less healthy alternative to home cooking. Eating out may seem like such a harmless activity, but it can quickly add up to hundreds of dollars per month, especially when you add extras like appetizers and alcoholic drinks at every meal.

My husband and I have established a monthly food budget that amounts to roughly one meal and a couple of coffees or lunch out per week. For us, eating out is a treat, and I am all about treats. But when you treat yourself every day, it ceases to be a treat and becomes a habit. Using your budget ahead of time, decide how much you can afford to treat yourself and make sure not to indulge too often lest it become the norm and your pockets remain empty.

Shopping

Speaking of treating yourself, this is the Achilles' heel for many of us, ladies. You must, must, *must* have some rules—or at least some general guidelines—about how much you will spend when it comes to shopping. Shopping gets out of hand quickly, especially if you've had a bad week at work or you're angry at your spouse or your children are acting like wild wolves. Sometimes you lose your mind and impulsively buy a pair of shoes on your way home from work to help yourself feel better. Been there, done that. Unfortunately, while impulsive decisions may feel great in the moment, in the long run they can have some pretty harsh consequences. Sit down and create your shopping rules before you find yourself in that situation.

I have a monthly "rolling budget" for shopping, so if I want to make a big purchase I skimp and save for several months. I also have a "must match three things" rule, which keeps me from buying clothes I never wear. Whenever I buy a nice piece of clothing, I have to be able to create three different outfits utilizing that item with other things in my closet. For some of you, this little rule may sound like a killjoy, but it has actually been incredibly helpful for me. It reduces the likelihood that I will buy lots of little dinky sale items that clutter up my closet and instead has helped me build a wardrobe of items that I can continually mix and match to create great outfits. Huzzah!

Back to the Budget

The common theme here is *budget*. Create a budget that allows you to live within your means. Then stick to it! I love online budgeting tools because they help me keep track of where my money is and where it's going. They also help me set goals and limitations on how and where I spend my money so I can meet my goals. As I noted at the beginning of this chapter, budgeting is a lot like exercising. You have to do it. And then do it again. And then again the next day. This is how good habits are built. You have to keep doing it for it to work.

Sometimes you fall off the wagon, eat a bunch of cake, and don't run for a couple of days because you have the flu or you just don't feel like it. It happens. But eventually you have to drag yourself out of bed and get right back on that stupid treadmill. If you keep at it long enough, eventually you will crest a hill and realize that you just paid off your credit card or that you have finally saved enough to make a down payment on a house. Look at you go!

If you'd like a little extra help getting started, check out this sample budget I pulled together, including notes below the chart that discuss each category.

Monthly Budget for a Single Gal Making $50,000 a Year

INCOME	Annually	Monthly	Notes
Gross Income	$50,000	$4,167	1
Taxes	-$10,000	-$833	2
After-Tax Income	$40,000	$3,333	3
EXPENSES			
Housing			
Rent	$12,000	$1,000	4
Utilities	$2,160	$180	5, 6
Phone	$720	$60	7
Transportation			
Car Payment	$3,600	$300	8
Gas	$1,800	$150	9
Insurance	$1,000	$83	10
Maintenance	$1,400	$117	11, 12

Food				
	Grocery	$3,120	$260	13
	Restaurants	$1,300	$108	14
	Coffee/Fast Food	$780	$65	15
Fun				
	Shopping	$600	$50	16
	Night Out	$600	$50	17
	Vacations	$1,500	$125	18
Health and Wellness				
	Gym Membership	$600	$50	19
	Doctor	$200	$17	20
	Dentist	$100	$8	20
Saving		$4,000	$333	21
Charity		$4,000	$333	22
TOTAL SPENDING		$39,480	$3,289	

Notes

1. "Gross" means before taxes.
2. I'm using a base estimate of 15 percent of your income for federal taxes and 5 percent for state taxes, but in reality taxes are very complex and vary from person to person. Use your own tax obligations here and don't neglect to include taxes in your budget because they are a legitimate expense.
3. Always build your budget using your net (after-tax) income because that is the actual amount you have to spend. If you already know what you're making after taxes, you can start with that number.
4. A good rule of thumb is that your total housing expense should equal roughly one-third or less of your total budget; if you live in a metropolitan area, finding affordable

housing may mean you need to find a roommate. Can you say "bunk beds?"

5. A survey of millennials by myfirstapartment.com found that on average, first-time renter's utility bills were roughly 18 percent of their rent. This includes cable and internet (see note 6).

6. At my house, we pay for Amazon Prime as an alternative to cable. As of this writing, the annual subscription was $100/year and includes additional benefits. A traditional cable package will cost anywhere from $20 to $80 a month depending on how many channels you want. A very basic internet package will cost around $50 per month, but some services will package cable and internet together which can help you save.

7. This is what I pay each month for a decent data package on an iPhone 6; my husband pays $10 per month for basic service and a very simple smartphone. Mobile phone bills can get out of hand quickly so be wary of "free phone deals." One way or another, you will almost always end up paying the full price of the phone—it may just be in the form of a "lease" or it may be built into the plan.

8. This would give you a very basic sedan that costs roughly $17,000 with a $2,000 down payment, paid off over five years with 2 percent interest. My first car out of college was a Honda Civic, and my payment was $254 per month.

9. This number can vary drastically depending on how much you drive and the price of gas where you live. This is a *very* general estimate based on filling up an average-size car once a week at an average cost of $35 per fill-up. If you commute a long distance, this number is probably too low.

10. This is roughly what my car insurance cost when I graduated college. It has gone down over the years; being a safe driver will save you hundreds over the course of your lifetime.

11. A survey by AAA suggests that you can plan to spend a little more than $1,400 on repairs, taxes, licensing, and car registration each year (obviously this number is higher if you drive a fancy car). It's tempting to ignore this category, but it's better for everybody if you don't. Flat tires and cracked windshields can be a huge drag on your spending—especially if you aren't prepared to pay for them.

12. I hope by now you're considering just how much you can save by using public transportation, especially if you live in a city and also have to pay for parking!

13. In their monthly survey, the USDA noted that a woman aged nineteen to fifty on a moderate budget spends roughly $260 per month on food at the grocery store. Try not to go too crazy on the steak and fancy wine and you should be OK.

14. This would give you $25 to spend each week on eating out at a nice restaurant. This may seem small, but remember, eating out is one of the quickest ways for you to bust your budget. If you'd like to spend more on eating out, recognize that you will have to spend less in other categories. Budgeting is a game of give and take.

15. This would give you $15 a week to spend on coffee with friends and/or lunch out. Again, eating out every meal is a surefire way to ruin your budget (and your health). Packing a lunch will save you thousands of dollars over your lifetime.

16. Like eating out, shopping is an area where you must

exercise self-control. I allow myself one nice outfit each month. If there's something high-end that I want, I skimp for a few months and save up for it.

17. Use this section of your budget for having fun with friends. Maybe that looks like catching a movie or two each month or going to see a concert. Just remember: if you treat yourself every night, it ceases to be a treat.

18. Every now and then a girl needs a vacation. Try to set aside a little bit each month so that you can take a nice trip somewhere each year without acquiring a ton of credit card debt.

19. This assumes a very basic membership of $50 per month (running outside is free!).

20. These numbers can also greatly vary depending on how healthy you are, your insurance plan, and how often you go to the doctor. But you shouldn't ignore these expenses. Make sure you're leaving room for annual checkups and preventive care.

21. A good starter savings goal is 10 percent of your salary that can initially be put toward building an emergency fund followed by saving for retirement and education (if you're wanting to continue your learning).

22. This may not be a line item for you; it is truly a matter of personal preference. I choose to budget 10 percent here. If this isn't important to you, then consider using this line as a space-holder for gift giving, saving up for a big purchase, or treating yourself to an extra vacation.

When Debt Is Good

Debt is often misused, but not all debt is bad. We live in an age of plentiful debt. With an adequate credit score, you can easily borrow money to buy a new car or purchase a home. You can borrow money to finance a new business idea or to go to college. In addition to using debt for large purchases, we also use debt to buy everything from a new pair of shoes to a cup of coffee. Think about it: every time you swipe your credit card, you are borrowing money to purchase something.

Debt is everywhere and while using debt has opened up a world of opportunity to us, it has also landed many of us in a world full of hurt. Too often I've heard stories of individuals who borrowed to buy a home they couldn't afford and ended up underwater (owing more than the home was worth). Then there's the seemingly harmless activity of rolling over credit card debt until the mounting interest makes the debt impossible to pay off, causing the debt holder to declare bankruptcy. But not all debt is bad. So when is it good?

Debt can be good when you are borrowing money with the intention of investing it in a way that will allow you to make *more* money or to buy an asset that is likely to increase in value. The key word here is *invest*. To help illustrate the important concept of using debt wisely, consider the following two examples.

Example 1: Let's say you own a retail clothing shop. Your shop is doing well, but you'd like it to grow. You currently sell about $500 of merchandise each day, and you use that money to pay your employees and buy new merchandise. However, you decide to borrow money to buy even more merchandise; with a larger inventory, you increase your sales so much that you are able to pay back the loan with interest and still pocket a little extra money. You have used debt to grow your business—in other words, you have used debt to successfully invest in your business. This is great news! You have used debt in a good way!

Example 2: Let's say you love to shop for clothes. Each month you have $100 to spend on new purchases. You'd really like to spend more, so you borrow $1,000 and go on a crazy shopping spree, spending the entire sum that you borrowed in one trip to the mall. But now the lender wants you to not only pay back the $1,000 you borrowed but to pay interest too, which means you owe more than $1,000. Unfortunately, you don't have the money, you did not make any money while shopping, and you did not make any purchases that could help you earn money to cover the interest. Now you have to borrow more money to pay off the first lender, and the second lender is going to charge you even more interest than the first one did, catapulting you into a cycle of ongoing debt. This is terrible news! You have used debt in a bad way!

The use of debt can help us grow the economic pie by providing capital to individuals with smart business ideas who lack the money to launch their ideas into the marketplace. Through both lending and borrowing, we can increase our opportunities to make money, which will leave both lender and borrower better off.

But trouble starts when we lend money for a poor idea that isn't likely to produce income or when we borrow for something that will not earn money. You're highly unlikely to ever earn money on new clothing, fun electronics, vacations, or elaborate weddings, so it's a bad idea to borrow money to pay for such things. Remember, if your purchase has no potential to earn money or increase in value, then it will not pay for the interest that accumulates if you can't pay back the debt immediately.

Food for Thought

Using credit cards to make purchases can sometimes be a smart idea if you use them to earn airline miles or reward points. But this works ONLY if you pay off your credit card each month. Do not allow your purchases to remain unpaid long enough to accumulate interest. Allowing unpaid balances to pile up on credit cards is the first step into bad debt.

On the flip side, houses and other real estate have the potential to increase in value, and earning a college diploma has the potential to get you a significantly better-paying job. Borrowing money to buy a home or pay for a college education can both be good uses of debt. But be careful to weigh the earnings potential against the amount you're borrowing. The potential increase in earnings or in value must outweigh the cost of the debt.

Credit Scores and Reports

Credit and debt are two sides of the same coin. In order for you to take on debt, someone else has to issue it. That someone else is a *creditor,* and they offer credit to you, the *debtor.* A credit report is like a debt report card. It includes items such as the amount of your current outstanding debt, your record on making payments on your debt, your address, and whether you've ever been sued, arrested, or filed for bankruptcy.[21] The report is compiled by a credit agency who can then provide it to potential lenders who are trying to decide whether or not to lend you money.

A credit score is based on the contents of the credit report. There are several methods for generating a score, which typically ranges from 300 to 850.[22] Ideally, you want to have a score higher than 700, which is considered good. Anything higher than 750 is excellent, while a score of 550 or below is cause for concern. Having a good credit score can make all the difference when it comes to renting or purchasing a home. In my experience, a good credit score helps assure landlords that you are responsible and will get your rent checks paid on time. Likewise, a mortgage loan officer views a high credit score as reassurance that you will make all scheduled payments on your loan, making them more likely to give you a mortgage with a lower interest rate.

A FICO score is a brand name for a credit score (like Kleenex is another name for tissues). The term comes from the company Fair Isaac Corporation, which created credit risk scoring in the 1960s.[23] In order to obtain a FICO score, you must have an account that has been open for at least six months, has been reported to the credit bureau, and doesn't belong to a deceased person (if you inherit an account you'll want to retitle it under your name).[24] You can improve your score by making sure to pay off your credit card balance each month and pay all your bills on time. The longer you maintain good credit, the higher your score will climb. That's why it's a good idea to open a credit card when you are able to make the payments so that you can start building credit.

As a consumer you are entitled to one free credit report from each of the three main credit reporting agencies (Equifax, Experian, and TransUnion) once every twelve months. After that you can pay for additional reports. It's a good idea to run a credit report for yourself at least once a year to check for signs of identity theft. To obtain a free report go to www.annualcreditreport.com.

Building a Game Plan for Paying Off Debt

Now that we have a good idea of when debt is helpful and when it's hurtful, let's talk about how to deal with prior decisions that have come back to haunt us. The first step to paying off debt is naming it and claiming it. You can't build a plan for paying off your debt if you refuse to acknowledge that you have debt. So start by making a list of all of your debt, noting the interest rate associated with each item. You can do this on a piece of paper or in a computer spreadsheet or other program. It's important that you gather everything in one place so you can begin to develop a game plan for paying off your debt.

Once you've made a list of everything you owe, rank your debt. Either rank your debt from the highest to lowest interest rate or in terms of the amount you owe. There are many methods you may choose to tackle your debts—pick one that works for you. Two of the most effective strategies are (1) to pay off your accounts in order of their interest rates, starting with the highest first; or (2) to pay off your accounts in order of the total amounts you owe, starting with either the smallest or the largest.

Using the first strategy, you will save money in the long run by not prolonging expensive interest payments. The longer you maintain debt with a high interest rate, the more you will pay, so it makes sense to first tackle the items that are costing you the most. However, following the second strategy allows you to pay off entire debts more quickly. This can give you a feeling of accomplishment sooner and also provide a sense of momentum. Of course, if you're like me and love a tough challenge, you may want to tackle the largest debt items first and work your way down. Taking that approach allows you to get the hardest stuff out of the way first, and you can be encouraged by knowing that it will only get easier.

Settle on a plan that makes sense to you. Once you've built a plan, stick with it. Consider giving yourself deadlines, rewarding yourself when you reach a milestone (without erasing the progress you made by racking up more debt!), or enlist the aid of a friend you trust who can help hold you accountable. Finally, if you're the type of person who needs to erase any hint of temptation, you might consider cutting up your credit cards and going credit-free during this process. I have a good friend who swears by a cash-only system; if that's what it takes to help you get back on track, then go for it. There's no shame in throwing out everything you've ever done in handling money and starting over with a new system.

Dealing with Student Debt

The student debt problem has garnered a lot of national attention in recent years. To give you an idea why it's such a hot topic, the Institute for College Access and Success notes that in 2013 seven in ten college seniors graduated with student debt, and the average amount of student debt was $28,400.[25] While the day-to-day cost of living in the U.S. (groceries, clothing, home goods, etc.) increases roughly 2 to 3 percent each year, the cost of obtaining a college education has historically risen 5 to 6 percent each year. Over the last seven years, my alma mater has increased its price tag from $52,000 per year to over $66,000 per year.[26] That's a $14,000 increase in less than a decade! Whether you're heading into college and looking at taking on student loans or on the other side of graduation trying to figure out how to pay them off, here are some helpful pointers on how to navigate the murky waters of student debt.

If you're currently applying to college, the best piece of advice I can give you is to consider beforehand how you will pay off any loans you might need to get through a particular school. It's easy to get caught up in the excitement and assume that you'll figure it all out later, but taking on tens of thousands of dollars in debt is a big deal, and you need to think long and hard before you do it. When you're starting college, you have no idea what the future holds. But here's a big question you should ask yourself: "Can I make the payments on the debt I'm undertaking in the career(s) I'm considering?" If you are planning on pursuing a degree such as accounting or engineering, your expected salary after you graduate might make it less risky to take on a large sum of debt. However, if you're planning on pursuing a degree such as creative writing or social work that typically offers less job security and lower pay, a huge pile of debt may make your path after graduation especially treacherous.

As previously discussed, debt is best used when it's put toward something expected to earn a good return (more money than you started with). So you must ask yourself if your likely income after college will provide a sufficient return to justify those loans. I love when people pursue their dreams, but too many people don't factor sizable student loans into their dream scenarios. That doesn't mean you have to pursue a degree in a field that bores you just because it tends to lead to higher-paying jobs. Perhaps you just need to reconsider what type of school you plan on attending and whether a prestigious name is worth extra debt. Your best return on investment might not be in the Ivy League.

If you're on the other side of the tassel and are now facing the overwhelming task of paying off debt, I suggest making a game plan for how you're going to do it. Having a feasible plan makes a world of difference when it comes to accomplishing financial goals. Start by looking at your budget and deciding how much you can afford to put toward that loan each month based on your income. Of course, your lender will insist on a minimum monthly payment, but if you can pay more than the minimum each month, you will crest that student loan mountain much sooner. Once you have a plan, keep an eye out for additional ways to pay off your loans even faster, because the quicker you pay them off, the less you will end up paying in interest. You might even consider taking a side job to help you get through them faster.

Food for Thought

If you have a lot of loans floating around out there, it might be a good idea to consolidate them. Some lenders may offer you a lower interest rate when you bundle your loans, and a lower rate means less money out of your pocket in the long haul. However, when it comes to consolidating loans, it's a good idea to consolidate private and government loans separately because government loans offer certain protections that you will lose if you lump them in with private loans.

How to Spend a Bonus

Use any bonuses you get to either pay down your student loans or other debts or to increase your long-term savings. The biggest factor to consider should be the interest rates on your student loans. If the interest rate on your debt is less than the return you could get by investing the money in the stock market, then you should invest it. By earning more you will be able to pay off more of the loan later on. To help clarify, consider the following hypothetical scenario.

Let's say you owe $1,000 that has an interest rate of 3 percent. You receive a $500 bonus this year and know you could invest it in a fund that will return an average of 5 percent per year after fees and taxes.* You could either apply your $500 to your debt now or apply it to your debt after it's earned some extra cash in the market.

Scenario 1: Apply Bonus Today

Time Frame	Debt	Invested Bonus
Today	$1,000 − $500 = $500	$500 − $500 = $0
Year 1	$500 × 1.03 = $515	$0
Year 2	$515 × 1.03 = $530	$0
Year 3	$530 × 1.03 = $546	$0
Total Owed	**$546**	

Scenario 2: Invest and Apply Bonus Later

Time Frame	Debt	Invested Bonus
Today	$1,000	$500
Year 1	$1,000 × 1.03 = $1,030	$500 × 1.05 = $525
Year 2	$1,030 × 1.03 = $1,061	$525 × 1.05 = $551
Year 3	$1,061 × 1.03 = $1,093	$551 × 1.05 = $579
Total Owed	$1,093 − $579 = **$514**	

* *The market earning 5 percent per year is a hypothetical scenario and not guaranteed.*

As you can see from the chart, because the market rate you can earn on your investment is higher than the interest rate on the debt you owe, you are able to pay off more of the debt in the long run if you invest the bonus now and use it to pay off your debt later. The math is simple enough, but you should also consider your own behavioral tendencies in this scenario. Often, people don't actually invest their bonus, stay the course, pull it out with a gain, and pay off the debt. Instead, they never invest the money in the first place (they splurge instead) or they put the money in the market but panic and sell out when the market falls (returns aren't guaranteed). If you're likely to follow either of those paths, then the math is irrelevant.

If you don't think you're disciplined enough to follow through with investing first and paying your debt later, consider splitting the difference. Put a portion of your bonus toward your debt right now and a portion toward some type of long-term savings (think retirement, a down payment on a home, an emergency fund, etc.). It's always a good idea to develop the habit of saving some portion of anything you make for the future.

To visualize your big financial picture, it helps to imagine two hypothetical piles that represent your personal balance sheet. One pile is a bad pile. This is your long-term debt—student loans, auto loans, home loans, etc. You want to make this pile go away. The other is a good pile. These are your assets—savings account, retirement accounts, home equity, etc. You want to make this pile grow because someday you will use this pile to buy a house, pay for a car, or retire. Your ongoing financial goal in life is to try to make the bad pile smaller and the good pile bigger because having many assets and few liabilities creates stability and makes most financial goals possible. When you get extra money in the form of a bonus, a gift, or a raise, put at least part of your windfall toward this dual goal of lessening your debt and increasing your assets. If you pursue these two objectives diligently, you'll be in a much better financial position in the long run.

PART 4

Personal Finance
at Home

I will look after you and I will look after anybody
you say needs to be looked after, any way you say.
I am here. I brought my whole self to you.
I am your mother.

—MAYA ANGELOU, *MOM & ME & MOM*

Whether you're an old momma, a new momma, a grand-momma, a single momma, a momma-to-be, or even a don't-wanna-be-a-momma, your approach to money at home significantly affects not only your financial achievement but also the health and well-being of your family. Hopefully you've realized by now that money has the potential to influence your self-confidence and your behavior, so it shouldn't come as a surprise that it also has the ability to influence your relationships.

In my own life, money is one of the things my spouse and I argue about the most, and I know that how we approach money will affect the way our children view it. Part 4 not only examines the logistics of dealing with money in the home, but it also explores ways to think about and talk about money with the other people in your home. The upcoming chapters will look at budgeting for a wedding, spousal IRAs, childcare costs, the Nanny Tax, and saving for college. But we'll also discuss the least-threatening ways to talk about money with your spouse and give you tips for raising financially savvy kids.

CHAPTER 8

Every Girl Needs
at Least Two Purses:
Advice on Money
and Marriage

WHEN I WAS A JUNIOR IN COLLEGE, I had coffee one evening with a scruffy-looking boy who bought most of his clothing at Goodwill and liked to walk around barefoot. For the next two years, I vacillated between hating him and loving him while he "thought of me as a sister." I am now married to that man, and these days he lets me buy him grownup clothing (although he still insists on cutting his own hair).

Shortly after we began dating, Tom invited me to drive home with him one weekend to meet his family. This very anxiety-producing event was made worse by the fact that we had to drive from Los Angeles to Phoenix before any awkward introductions could take place. If you have been to Los Angeles, then you know that it is full of people who like to drive by themselves on streets that were at capacity several decades ago. Driving through the City of Angels at any time is awful. Driving through it at rush hour is a nightmare.

On this first road trip together, we hit traffic about fifteen minutes in, and for the next two hours we inched our way through Los Angeles. When Tom is frustrated about something, his lips disappear into his face. By the time we made it to the other side of Los Angeles on this trip, Tom had consumed most of his face, a sign that he was quite grumpy. Unfortunately for both of us, our conversation somehow made its way to the category of "belongings and shopping habits" in general and purses in particular.

Personally, I think shopping is a sport that should be elevated to Olympic status because I would be a gold medal contender. I also believe a girl should have at least two purses: a black one and a brown one. But you probably also need a cream one, a clutch, one with a shoulder strap, one to cradle on your forearm, one that can hold an entire meal, one that can hold nothing but a $5 bill and some lip balm, and a second black one in case the first black one isn't the right shape for your outfit. Essentially, a purse for every major occasion in life. Tom does not share my view of the need for purses. At the time, I was in possession of roughly four purses—a number that I thought was well under my maximum limit and that Tom thought was beyond excessive.

Maybe it was because we were tired or maybe because our vision had been blurred by the red taillights we had followed for hours, but in that moment the process of purchasing purses became a hotly contested topic. The "purse fight" and other discussions soon made clear that my new boyfriend and I viewed the act of spending money in very different ways. All my life, I have considered myself to be a moderate saver. Throughout college I slowly socked away a tiny amount of savings and proudly made all of my car and credit card payments on time. By the time I graduated, I had managed to save roughly $2,000 in my checking account. Considering the fact that I had graduated from an absurdly expensive school debt-free (with the help of scholarships and my savings-savvy parents), I believed myself to be a very wealthy twenty-two-year-old.

After Tom and I were engaged, we shared our personal net worth while strolling along the beach one fine afternoon. I proudly announced the chunk of change I had sitting in my checking account, but instead of exclaiming, "Wow! That's great," my future husband became silent. I wasn't sure what to think about this unexpected response, until he quietly said, "I've saved up about forty thousand." As it turns out, not only was Tom excellent at not spending money, but he was excellent at investing it. He had not only saved the majority of his income from various jobs since he was around twelve years of age, but he had also been investing it in the stock market and had reaped the benefits of contributing money during one of the best market run-ups in history. (If you don't believe in the benefits of compounding returns, you should have a chat with my husband).

Days (let's be honest, months) later, when the shock finally wore off, I felt incredibly blessed and downright lucky to have married such a "wealthy" man. But at that moment on our beach walk, all I felt was embarrassed and inadequate. By comparison, I was bringing nothing to the marriage. My offering was so tiny compared to his that it would take me years to make up that gap and finally put us on even ground.

But here's what I needed to learn then and want to tell you now: marriage should *never* be about keeping score—especially on money issues. When we rank ourselves in our relationships as better or worse based on our bank account or our spending habits or our paychecks, we miss out on the chance to love and be deeply loved for who we are and not because of what we have.

Over the years, Tom and I have both taken one for the team and ridden on the coattails of the other. For a season, Tom worked hard while I took time off to study for the Chartered Financial Analyst exams (they say each of the three exams requires roughly 300 hours of studying to pass and I can vouch for that). Later, Tom quit his job, and I began pulling more of the financial weight so he could go to grad school. We expect that we will continue to take income-earning turns for years and years to come; whose turn it is will not be dictated by who went last, or who gave the most for the longest, but by who is in need of a change of pace and who is in a position to lovingly give so that the other may receive. We did not come to this spot easily; it required purposeful conversation and decisions about our earning and our spending habits and our priorities for our marriage and family.

Talking about money is hard. Talking about money with your spouse may be the hardest conversation you will have. For Tom and me, how we handle money is an ongoing conflict because our habits and views diverge so extremely in this area. Even though these conversations can be difficult, we choose to talk about money frequently because we value our marriage and want to nurture and strengthen it. Each time we have a serious conversation, it gets a little bit easier. We are both learning to find value in the other's spending habits. I find myself more frequently questioning my purchases: Do I really need that extra throw pillow? Is that blouse something I must have? How can I spend money in a way that demonstrates love for others? And slowly but surely, Tom is learning to appreciate my love of soft, cozy things and my desire to create a warm and inviting resting place for our friends and family.

It's not easy to have conversations about how you choose to spend and save money, but I believe those conversations are deeply valuable—not just because they will give you a foundation for saving and spending, but also because those conversations will allow you to build that foundation together. When you make your decisions through teamwork, your partnership will be more likely to grow and flourish throughout life's different phases and purchases.

How to Talk about Money with Your Spouse

Taking the time to sit down and talk about your finances periodically with your spouse can really benefit the health of your marriage. It will also ensure that both spouses understand the financial state of the family in case of death or divorce. I've heard far too many stories about a surviving spouse who has no clue about where the couple's money was invested or who to call for details. While it can be incredibly intimidating to sit down and talk about who is spending what and whether you can save more, consider the following tips and tricks to make the conversation easier and more productive.

Talk about how *you* prefer to spend money, how your family spent money when you were growing up, and how you feel about spending certain sums of money. Money isn't just about math. It's also about emotions because finances are intimately linked to your values. So before you even begin talking about the numbers with your spouse, lay out your preferences and your expectations.

The "purse fight" was a good example of how *not* to have

a good conversation about money. Fortunately, since then, Tom and I have learned how to have better conversations about shopping habits and our expectations for ourselves and each other. Understanding how you and your spouse think about making purchases will help you better understand how and why each of you spends money. I like to buy things that are pretty. My husband likes to buy things that are useful. Understanding each other's preferences helps us better budget our money so we both get what we want—at least some of the time. Taking the time to communicate expectations and preferences can take some of the pressure off the conversation.

Create a budget. Together. I cannot emphasize enough the importance of having a budget. (Yes, I know we already talked about this in the last chapter, but that's how important I think this is!) A budget helps prevent you from making regrettable, impulsive purchases, and it helps you save for your goals.

Establishing a budget you can both agree on will be the hardest part of the conversation—and the part most likely to cause arguments. But the long-term benefits of having a budget that you both created—and believe in using—are immense. Budget for daily, weekly, monthly, and yearly expenses. And don't forget to budget for things that each of you enjoy. It's also a good idea to save for family goals, such as a vacation or a house. When you have a mutual goal that you can both contribute to and benefit from, you're more likely to save for that goal.

Food for Thought

One great way to create a budget you can agree on is to create his and her "buckets" for discretionary spending. A couple I know delegates $100 to each spouse monthly. He typically spends his money on outdoor equipment while she spends hers on clothing. Because it is a "no-questions-asked" bucket, they avoid tense arguments about which purchases are frivolous or silly.

Create an "emergency contacts" list for your money. This list is particularly helpful if one spouse manages the majority of the household finances. Sit down together and create a list of all your accounts, where they're located, how much is in each one, and who to call in the event of an emergency. That way, the less financially involved spouse has at least a basic understanding of where the money is and who to call if something happens.

Planning a Super Awesome Wedding on a Budget

An excellent way to establish a peaceful, productive financial relationship in your marriage is to begin by planning your wedding together. I am passionate about wedding planning from a financial standpoint because I am passionate about healthy relationships. According to the website costofwedding.com, the average U.S. couple spends $26,645 on their wedding.[27] That's a lot of money.

Because I was a bride myself not so long ago, I know that it's easy to get so caught up in planning the perfect day that you lose sight of the real objective: to get married. When planning a wedding becomes all about the wedding, the pressure to have everything play out perfectly can wreak havoc on your mental health and your relationships. Hence, my first wedding planning tip is this: make wedding planning about your *marriage* and not about the wedding itself.

I enjoy weddings because they almost always involve dessert and dancing—two things I love with my whole heart. I don't want to sound prideful, but my wedding was the best wedding that ever happened (after Kate Middleton's of course). It was a perfect day full of partying with my favorite people, and by the time it was over, I was married to my best friend, which was the end goal after all. Your wedding can also be the best wedding ever, and to help you get there, I've compiled some helpful suggestions to keep your wedding planning on point and under budget.

Work to Your Strengths

Some grooms do not care what color the napkins are or how many roses you carry in your bouquet. Others (like my husband) want to be involved in every decision. Either way, it's OK! Whatever type of future spouse you have, it's important to involve them in some way. Marriage is full of celebrating joyful things and making hard decisions, which makes wedding planning a good crash course in preparing for marriage. Use this time to learn how to function as a team with your significant other. Your special day will be more meaningful when you've brought it to fruition together.

Like I said earlier, weddings are expensive. If you haven't figured that out yet, you're about to. Before options like plated dinners and dance floor rentals unexpectedly plow through your wallet, sit down and make a budget. Don't just pick a number and call it a day. Make sure that number is realistic. Do your research. Break out every little expense you could possibly expect to have and allocate some of your budget to it. Make sure to include things like taxes and tipping because those are real costs, and if you don't include them you will undoubtedly go over your budget.

Wedding planner websites such as theknot.com can help you with their built-in calculators and can provide estimates for certain items and services. Make sure to review your budget with anyone who is helping cover the cost of the wedding. It's better to discuss these things up front than surprise mom and dad with your expectations later. (Trust me on this one!)

Food for Thought

Don't go into the bridal store planning to spend $1,000 on a dress and leave with a $10,000 dress. That's a big no-no. Just because every other girl on *Say Yes to the Dress* does that doesn't make it OK. You can find a gorgeous dress within your budget; to prevent temptation, simply ask the attendant not to pull out any dresses that are outside of your budget. In the long run, you will be really thankful you did.

Set Priorities and Make Good Choices

Once you have your budget, stick to it, but be willing to be flexible on individual line items as you go. If your caterer ends up costing more than you expected, look through your budget for ways to cut expenses in other categories. Consider the following cost-cutting ideas that can help save your wallet while still allowing you to throw an awesome wedding. I know because I used them.

Consider a buffet or family style meal. Plated catering is really expensive because you have to pay for extra labor to "plate" the meal for all of your guests. More labor means more money. We shaved thousands of dollars off our catering bill by providing a buffet style dinner that was still delicious and really classy.

- *Consider picking a set number of beverages instead of offering an open bar.* My husband and I were married at a golf club associated with a vineyard, which allowed us to order alcoholic beverages in bulk directly from their suppliers, which made it quite a bit cheaper. The woman in charge of the venue offered this great piece of advice: *your guests don't know what they're missing; they only know what's offered to them.* Don't worry about having every different kind of drink under the sun available to your guests. They're just happy to be there celebrating with you, and they're happy to eat and drink whatever you're offering.

- *Figure out what you can do yourself.* I have a crafty momma, and we decided to make our own table centerpieces. The day before my wedding we got up early and drove to the Los Angeles Flower Market (which is an amazing place to visit even if you aren't planning a wedding) and bought a ton of flowers for about $200. The Flower Market is where florists purchase flowers at a significant discount from the retail florist prices, so when I say a ton I mean a ton. They were fresh and absolutely gorgeous the day of the wedding. On the flip side, you also want to know your limitations. I can arrange some flowers in a vase just fine, but I know nothing about bouquets, corsages, or boutonnieres. We paid a lovely woman to pull those flowers together for us, and she did an excellent job.

- *Get creative when it comes to attire.* I was lucky enough to have a mother who had good taste in the 1980s, and with the help of a lot of cardio and an amazing seamstress, I was able to wear her wedding dress with slight modifications to give it a modern look. I got to wear a gorgeous silk dress for a fraction of what a similar new dress would have cost me. Plus, wearing the dress was a special way to honor the close friendship I have with my mom and cross off "something old and something borrowed" from the list. Instead of renting a tux for my groom, we purchased a nice gray suit for him to wear. It ended up costing only a little bit more than renting a tux, and now he has a custom-tailored suit that he can wear for a multitude of other occasions.

- *Make friends with talented people.* This is where we saved the most and honestly had the most fun. Our photographer was a dear friend of my husband's and has since become such a good friend to both of us that she is responsible for the wonderful design of my financial planning blog, The Cupcake Club, and the photo on the cover of this very book. She was kind enough to gift us her services as a wedding present. Not only did we save on photography, but we had a ton of fun shooting our pictures because we did it surrounded by friends. When it came time to dance, we loaded up an iPod with our favorite tunes and handed it off to a friend who served as an impromptu DJ. Not only did we save money, but we had the most epic dance party.

- *Last, but not least, don't skimp on the cake.* No one likes a dry cake.

If you're stepping into your own wedding planning journey, know that I am so very excited for you! The process might feel overwhelming at times, but I promise you it's totally worth it. I hope your wedding is every bit as fun and joy-filled as mine was. And I also hope that you find ways to make your wedding special that don't involve taking on debt that will haunt you for years to come. If you're looking for additional resources for wedding planning, I highly recommend poking around theknot.com. In the meantime, congratulations and good luck!

CHAPTER 9

Motherhood and Raising Financially Savvy Kids

A S I SIT WRITING THIS CHAPTER, I am just shy of eleven weeks pregnant. For now, it's a cherished secret reserved for family and close friends. For about a month I was under the impression that pregnancy was really easy. I felt great! I had plenty of energy. I was a steam-engine of productivity. I even managed a hectic work trip to Chicago that involved little sleep and a ton of walking. Sadly, about two weeks before I was scheduled to sit for the third level of the Chartered Financial Analyst exam, I began to feel nauseated and exhausted. I spent the better part of each day asleep on the floor. When I started throwing up, my secret was out of the bag.

I hate throwing up. I have made it a lifelong goal not to throw up. Morning sickness was a very misleading term for this affliction. I once threw up all over my kitchen at 11 p.m. That's not the morning! I also hate feeling tired. I'm a doer. I want to be productive. Shortly after we found out I was pregnant, we moved into a new home and I wanted to paint and clean and furnish. I wanted to nest. I wanted to finish this bloody book. Instead I napped every three hours and rarely showered before noon. I was my own worst nightmare.

For as long as I can remember, I wanted to be a powerhouse career woman. I wanted to sit at a glass desk on the forty-fourth floor and work until midnight. I wanted to pace the floor in beige-colored boardrooms flanked by floor-to-ceiling windows. I wanted a life that moved so fast the only way to handle it would be to consume copious amounts of caffeine. Yet here I am—at home, in workout gear that hasn't seen sweat in weeks, cuddled under a *Frozen* blanket while it drizzles outside, surprisingly at peace with the way my life has played out. In many ways, I am a "nobody." I work at a tiny company and live in the suburbs. I have fewer than a thousand friends on Facebook.

Still, I have never felt so powerful. A teeny tiny person is growing inside of me. No power suit or high-rise office could ever make me feel so confident, so certain of my abilities. A teeny tiny heart is nestled below mine, and it's beating ever so delicately, and someday I will get to peer into the eyes of the owner of that heartbeat and proclaim that this tiny person is so deeply loved and valued. I am surprisingly content to give up my childish notions of a powerhouse career for such a sweet gift. (My daughter, Brené, has since arrived and upended my world, but more on that later.)

I want to acknowledge that many women out there aren't as lucky as I am and that many others have chosen a different path. Please know that whether your path is similar to mine or completely different, I'm glad you're on it—so long as it is healthy and brings you happiness of course. And I also want to acknowledge that there are many different yet valuable approaches to motherhood. Motherhood is getting manis and pedis with my mom and daughter and watching

Gilmore Girls while we drink steaming cups of hot tea, but it's also my piano teacher who has welcomed hundreds of neighborhood children in for dachshund kisses and pieces of chocolate before their lessons. Motherhood can be the aunt who spoils her nieces and nephews or the teacher who brings in extra hats and gloves for students in need. Motherhood at its core is nurturing little ones in a scary world, and we so desperately need all different kinds of mothers. Nurturing children is a sacred activity, and I wish we would appreciate that more and criticize less.

I've heard the criticism poured out on women: If you choose to work you're being selfish. If you choose to stay at home you're setting a bad example for your children. I've seen the stories about how women can have it all, but I find that idea simply exhausting. You can't have it all. You can't work the power job, raise a family of brilliant, talented children, go to the gym every day, cook every meal from scratch, keep a perfect home, and stay sane. Life is wonderfully messy, and it's OK.

Furthermore, what I choose and what you choose can both be the right choices. We don't have to spend our days judging and criticizing each other to prove our own approach to womanhood is the correct one. What we can do is choose to offer each other grace and support the different choices we make as women. We can encourage each other; being a woman—much less a mother—can be hard, but feeling like you have a team behind you makes a world of difference. Let's be proud of ourselves because we are doing the best that we can and that is enough.

This chapter is a battle cry that women who nurture children are doing jobs of great importance, and I refuse to let the world tell us differently. Mothers matter, and this chapter is all about ways that you, as a mother, can be savvy with your money—and raise your children to be savvy, too.

Tough Love Can Lead to Lifelong Gratitude

When I was growing up, my parents made it a point to involve my brother and me in the family finances—especially as those finances related to each of us. One of the ways I think they did really well in teaching us about money was to slowly increase our financial responsibilities. They started by giving us an allowance beginning when we were in elementary school. It was a weekly amount (something like $10), but it came with strings attached: in order to receive the allowance we had to complete daily chores such as making our bed or washing the dishes. At the time I hated chores (like most children), but now I'm thankful that they taught me that there are few handouts in life and that if you want something you need to work for it.

At the age of eight, I asked my mom if I could take piano lessons. Music lessons of any kind can quickly become a very expensive endeavor; by the time I was in high school my lessons cost more than $100 a week. Luckily, my mom foresaw how expensive it would become and from the beginning made sure I was committed by making me pay a portion of the lesson fee whenever I didn't practice beforehand. At the time it felt cruel (that seems to be a pattern), but in hindsight I'm so thankful she insisted on that arrangement. Having taught piano myself, I know how pointless it is to try to teach a child who doesn't practice and have seen what a waste of money that can be for parents.

Food for Thought

Take a lesson from my mother. Whatever activity your child chooses to pursue, find a way to make them feel invested. Require them to pay for a portion of specialized equipment with their allowance. Or be like my mother and make your kids chip in to pay for a wasted lesson when they don't practice. Doing so ties them financially to the activity and encourages them to work hard and learn self-discipline.

When I turned sixteen and acquired a driver's license, my dad decided it was time for me to get a job. He then made sure I got one by refusing to pay for my gas. Again, this felt unfair at the time, but, of course, I am grateful in hindsight. With each passing year, my parents paid less and less of my personal expenses. When I turned seventeen they quit paying for my entertainment. If I wanted to see a movie, I had to buy the ticket with my own earnings. When I left for college, they gave the family car I had been driving to my brother. If I wanted a car, I had to buy my own. By my junior year of college, I was responsible for all of my food and discretionary spending, and the instant I graduated, I was handed the bill for my car insurance.

With each new responsibility I was given, I became less and less grumpy about how mean my parents were and more and more thankful for the lessons they had taught me in self-sufficiency. My transition to adulthood wasn't nearly as painful as what many of my peers experienced because I already had a pretty good grasp of my living expenses and was prepared to pay them.

From the time your child is about five or six, you can teach them lessons about how to be smart with money. It will probably be difficult. They will probably fight you, but by including them in their own expenses, you're giving them the gift of self-sufficiency. One day they'll thank you (and you'll thank you).

How to Save for Retirement When You Don't Bring in a Paycheck

One of the best ways to raise financially savvy children is to model financially savvy behavior. Many women put off saving for their own retirement because they are so busy raising their kids and saving for college educations. Don't get so busy or focused on your offspring that you neglect your own financial needs. Saving for your own retirement is smart, and we should all want to set smart examples for our kids.

Saving for retirement is also difficult, especially if you leave the workforce to care for your children. Usually, such a move requires you to give up valuable retirement benefits offered by employers. The work you're doing at home is immensely valuable, but let's face it, little Jimmy doesn't offer any 401(k) matching contributions for changing his diapers.

Of course, you could argue that your spouse is saving for the both of you—which is great! After all, you're saving the family tens of thousands of dollars a year in childcare costs alone. But personally, I think it's always helpful in a marriage to feel like you are part of a team, and it's good for your children to see you taking care of your own needs.

That's why I encourage mommas everywhere to actively take part in saving for retirement. The good news is that you have a couple of viable options to help you save.

Spousal IRAs

All you have to do to be eligible for a spousal IRA is file a joint tax return. Once you've checked that box, you can open a traditional or a Roth IRA with the blessings of the IRS. (See chapter 6 for more details on retirement accounts and whether you should open a traditional or Roth). There are limits to your contributions based on your age and your family income, so check with your tax advisor to find out the details. And remember, every little bit counts—even if you can only add a few dollars a month to your account.

SEP IRAs

If you're a "mompreneur" or a mommy blogger (which is very in vogue these days), there's more great news! As long as you report your home-based business on your tax return, you can also set up a self-employed 401(k), also known as an SEP IRA. This option allows you to contribute significantly more than the spousal IRA as the contribution limit is the lesser of 25 percent of your income or $53,000 (for 2016).[28] And, if you're feeling particularly savings aggressive, you can contribute to your SEP from your business earnings and still contribute to a traditional or Roth IRA.

How Smart Mommas Save for College

The two best gifts I've received in my life to date are a piano from my grandmother when I was thirteen and a college education. I always had wonderful piano teachers who encouraged public performance, and my Grandma Fritzie came to every concert. About the time I turned thirteen, I found myself heavily immersed in music—singing, composing, playing in little quartets made up of other awkward thirteen-year-olds. I had found my calling, and my wonderful grandma noticed.

After a particular middle school orchestra concert that featured me as a soloist to an embarrassing extent, my grandma decided that I needed a real piano. The next day, my mom and my piano teacher took me to pick out a piano. I chose a gorgeous cherry upright, and I have loved that beautiful piano ever since. That incredible gift demonstrated to me that my grandma had recognized my passion and that she believed in it. She was and always will be my greatest fan.

A few years later, when I began applying for college, my parents made a deal with me. I could go wherever I wanted, provided I made up the difference in cost between wherever I went and a state school, which they were prepared to pay for. I was incredibly blessed to receive a partial scholarship to Pepperdine University, and after spending four years in paradise, I graduated debt-free. This was the second most humbling gift I have ever received, and it's still easy to take it for granted.

Fortunately, my close proximity to financial news prevents me from forgetting how many students are laden with debt by the time they graduate college. Consequently, I am so very thankful to my parents for planning ahead. From the moment I was born, they were in my corner, preparing for my future, rooting for my success. I consider my parents' contribution to my college education one of the many ways they invested in me and let me know how much they cared.

Start Early

Ultimately, it's up to you to decide whether you will pay for or contribute to your kids' college education. But know that helping pay those costs can be an incredible gift. As the cost of a college education continues to skyrocket, it has become increasingly important for you to start early and save efficiently if you want to make a dent in those tuition bills. According to the College Board, the organization that provides college entrance exams, average tuition costs currently range from $16,325 a year for public two-year colleges to $46,272 a year for private four-year institutions.[29] If you consider that inflation for higher education costs has been historically around 6 percent, then in sixteen years, you could be looking at paying $121,078 per year in tuition.[30] At $121,078 a year, it could cost $484,312 to send your now-toddler to a private college! Even if we assume a base case scenario of 3 percent inflation, you're still looking at around $75,000 per year in tuition, and that's not including additional costs like books, fees, and room and board. While it may be easy to cross your fingers and hope your child will receive a handsome scholarship, it's probably more realistic to start saving now for little Jimmy's dream school—just in case.

Like saving for any other long-term goal, the earlier you start saving for college the better. By starting early, you allow yourself a longer time frame for your savings to grow.

Special Education Savings Accounts

Several types of educational savings accounts can help your dime go farther than it would if you chose to just stash money in a sock drawer or a savings account at the bank. The most common and arguably the easiest to use are called 529 accounts, followed by Education Savings Accounts (ESAs). These accounts, which have slightly different rules, allow you to save for higher education by investing in a variety of securities without having to pay taxes on the investment gains. The following is a summary of each kind of account provided by Vanguard.[31]

	Education Savings Accounts	529s
Who Can Contribute	Anyone who meets the income level restrictions can contribute to the account	Anyone can contribute to the account regardless of income level
Income Restrictions	Individual contribution limits are reduced and gradually phased out (for modified AGI of $95,000 and $110,000 if single and $190,000 and $220,000 if married filing jointly)	There are no income level restrictions
Contribution Limits	Total annual contributions cannot exceed $2,000	No limits, but gift tax rules apply
Eligible Expenses	Qualified education expenses (including books, tuition, and supplies) at private elementary and secondary schools, and private and public higher education including graduate school	Qualified education expenses (including books and tuition) at private elementary and secondary schools (up to $10,000), and private and public higher education including graduate school
Tax Benefits	Account value grows tax free	Account value grows tax free Some states allow you to deduct part or all of your contributions

Age Restrictions	Contributions can only be made until the beneficiary turns 18 and only remain tax-free until the beneficiary turns thirty	Most 529 plans have no age restrictions
Risks	Most investment choices are not FDIC-insured and are subject to relevant investment risks	Most investment choices are not FDIC-insured and are s ubject to relevant investment risks
Penalty	Earnings not spent on education incur a 10 percent federal tax penalty	Earnings not spent on education incur a 10 percent federal tax penalty
Transferability	Assets can be transferred to other eligible family members	Assets can be transferred to other eligible family members

The 529 accounts are typically the most popular choice largely because they allow you to contribute more than $2,000 per year, which is the limit on ESAs. If you're hesitant to use a 529 or an ESA because you don't want to lock up your money (there is a tax penalty for spending it on anything other than education), consider the following example.

Let's say that in eighteen years you want to be able to send your daughter to a public school for four years without having to take out any debt. Assuming 3 percent inflation and moderate returns, you would need to save roughly $3,300 each year in a 529 account. If you choose to save in a regular taxable account instead, you would need to save closer to $3,900 each year because of the additional taxes you would have to pay on the growth of those investments. Consequently, you end up saving roughly $600 each year for the next eighteen years simply by *employing a tax-friendly 529. It also helps to know that 529s can be rolled over to other family members; so, if your daughter gets a scholarship and doesn't end up needing the full amount you've saved for her, you can use that money for any of her siblings.*

Food for Thought

If your child has already started college, make sure to take advantage of education credits when tax time rolls around. As of this writing, both the American Opportunity Tax Credit and the Lifetime Learning Credit offer tax breaks for individuals who are paying tuition at eligible institutions. Not everyone qualifies (typically due to income limits) so check with your tax-preparer regarding these tax breaks.

CHAPTER 10

Paying for Child Care

THE TRANSITION TO MOTHERHOOD was anything but simple for me. From the beginning, I had mixed feelings about maternity leave. In a small company like ours, losing the work of one person has a significant impact on our ability to function, and I didn't want to let my team or our clients down. Plus, I love to work and I really enjoy my job.

It came as no surprise then when my boss told me to take all the time I needed and hours after giving birth I was texting him to remind him of some outstanding actions. Two days later I was trading and answering emails. I felt guilty when the midwives would stop by to weigh the baby and ask when I was going back to work. I would lie and say "in a month or two" because I didn't want them to think I had a horrible boss when I was the one choosing to work instead of rest. But for me, doing even an hour of work every day or two was crucial to my postpartum healing. Taking care of details in a sphere where I was confident grounded me when it seemed like everything else in my world had turned upside down.

Of course, over time it became harder to work. The baby demanded more attention and eventually my husband had to return to his job full-time. Five months after my daughter was born, I started dropping her off with grandma and another part-time sitter six hours a day, four days a week, and while every goodbye is hard, I know that this time apart is good for both of us. She gets to learn how to socialize and I can better focus on my job.

I know that not everyone has the flexibility that I do, and I feel insanely lucky. I work from home, which is mostly wonderful but has its fair share of drawbacks. I miss out on "water cooler" conversations and don't get to attend as many client meetings as I used to, but I also get to make my job work for my company and our clients, and my family and our finances.

I could go on and on about the complexities of being a "working mom," but the truth is that the picture looks different for every mother, and there are no perfect solutions that fit every situation. The best advice I can offer is this:

1. Love your kids.
2. Work for someone who cares about you and your ability to love your kids.
3. Allow life to be messy.

My boss knew I would work even during my official maternity leave. But every few weeks he reminds me that this time with my baby is precious and encourages me to take the time I need to enjoy her. And so I do. I work early and late. I work weekends and during her naps. But sometimes I set the work down and cuddle with my girl or simply sit and watch her chest rise and fall while she sleeps. I take long lunches, and we play and run errands together. I allow my house to be cluttered, my hair to be dirty, and my life to be messy, and I am arranging childcare on my terms so that I can learn to be a mother while still helping my company and my bank account thrive.

I don't have a perfect solution to the working mom struggle, but I think it involves a lot of give and take and a lot of self-grace. And hopefully more and more employers will learn that being flexible will allow them to retain the talent of strong, hard-working mommas.

Nannies

When my husband and I were first researching childcare options, we contemplated hiring a part-time, in-home nanny. I was hesitant to send my child elsewhere when I had the ability to stay home and local daycares were too expensive for our budget. As I delved into different childcare sites, I discovered I would need to pay taxes for an in-home nanny.

The Nanny Tax falls under the topic of household help. You may not know this, but anyone who provides services to you in your own home may be considered an employee of your household. This makes you an employer subject to employer-related taxes. A key part of determining whether someone is an employee is your level of discretion over how they do their job. If you dictate how the job will be performed, the individual you are paying is an *employee*. If you dictate the results you want to obtain, the individual may be considered a *contractor*.

When it comes to childcare, the IRS lays out the following guidelines to help determine whether a nanny is an employee that you need to pay employer taxes for:
- You pay your worker more than $2,000 each year.
- The worker is not your parent, spouse, or child over the age of twenty-one.
- The worker is over eighteen.
- The worker provides care in your home.

- You tell the worker how to do the work. For example, someone from a cleaning service is not your employee but an employee of the service. However, a housekeeper you hire directly would be your employee.

If your household help meets these guidelines, you may owe taxes for Social Security, Medicare, and federal unemployment. You may be tempted to try to pay your nanny or housekeeper "under the table," but if you ever let them go and they try to file for unemployment benefits, you may be charged with tax evasion. To learn more about the rules regarding household help, check out the IRS webpage on the topic.

After calculating what we would have to pay in taxes and recognizing the added benefits of not having my daughter distracting me from the next room, we decided to employ relatives and a family friend to provide care from their respective homes.

Daycare

According to Care.com, the average annual cost of a reputable daycare in 2016 was $10,972.[32] For a dual-income home earning over six figures, this may not be a huge inconvenience, but for many individuals it's often cheaper for one spouse to simply stay home than to pay for daycare—especially as their family grows. Of course, that means significantly cutting your household income—sometimes by half—which may make things tight.

Another downside of traditional daycare is a lack of flexibility. Given that I work from home and that my husband is a graduate student, we wanted a daycare option that was flexible so we could drop our daughter off when we both needed to work and pick her up when one of us was available to watch her. Most daycares we investigated would charge for a full workweek regardless of how much time a child spent there. A friend recommended that I should look into in-home daycares.

Unlike traditional daycare operations that operate from a commercial place of business, in-home daycares are offered by a licensed professional inside an individual's home. Because the provider doesn't have to pay all the expenses of a commercially based daycare (rent, utilities, and certain admin fees) they typically charge less. You might also find this option gives you greater peace of mind if you can find an in-home daycare run by someone you know or have been personally referred to. The neighborhood discussion website Nextdoor can be a good place to start if you're looking for local in-home daycares.

Another alternative to traditional daycare is a nanny share. This option offers the benefits of a nanny but allows you the split the costs with other families. As the name implies, a nanny share involves finding other families with similar needs and hiring a nanny to look after all of your children. You typically have to pay the nanny more over-all because of the larger number of children, but because you're divvying up the costs this option usually ends up being cheaper than hiring a nanny on your own. The hard part (for us at least) was finding a family with similar needs.

As I've mentioned before, we ended up creating a piece-meal approach to childcare that gives us affordability and flexibility. For us, this means my mom watches our daughter several days a week and a family friend with a toddler watches her other days. We pay the family friend on an hourly basis, and we pay for my mom's monthly manicures and pedicures. All in all it ends up costing us around $600 a month.

CHAPTER 11

Wills and Trusts

A S MY HUSBAND AND I prepared to welcome our first child, we wanted to make sure to set up a proper will and a living trust. While preparing a will can sound like a very morbid activity, knowing your affairs are in order can bring great security. Regardless of your marital or parental status, creating a will is a crucial step in making sure your loved ones will be taken care of if something happens to you.

Having a will allows you to decide how you want your estate to be disbursed after you've passed and who will care for any minor children. While we all hope to live long, healthy lives, there are no certainties. Personally, I can celebrate my daughter more knowing that if anything were to happen to my husband and me, she would be cared for by someone that we trust and have handpicked to raise her. Furthermore, having a will can help your successors avoid a lengthy probate process in court. Probate is the legal process of deciding what will happen to your estate once you have passed, and having a clearly written will can help streamline the proceedings.

An additional benefit of having a will is that it ensures that your estate does not pass to someone you'd rather not pass it to. While setting up a will requires some effort, it can easily be amended later as your life situation changes, ensuring that you can add new children and remove ex-spouses should the need arise.

Living Trusts

Once you have a will in place, you may want to also consider the benefits available from having a trust. Trusts are ideal for individuals who have accumulated a substantial amount of wealth and want to add an additional level of protection for that money. A properly executed trust should also allow you to avoid probate.

For our purposes here, we'll focus on living trusts, which are much more relevant to the average individual's situation. A living trust allows you to maintain control over the trust while you're living and appoint someone to succeed you as trustee after you die, which gives you the greatest level of control over money placed in the trust and what happens to it. A living trust can be nullified, changed, or amended at any time. You choose which assets to place in the trust; anything inside the trust is governed by its dictates while anything you leave outside of the trust becomes subject to your will.

You may not think you need a trust if you have a well-written will. But if you die, assets above a certain amount—called a *de minimis*—will become subject to probate. This amount varies by state, but to give you an idea of how much it is, as of 2017 the California *de minimis* amount was $150,000 and the Colorado *de minimis* amount was $64,000.[33] The following example can help you understand why this could be an issue.

You have established a will in which you have dictated where you want all your assets to go. You then create a trust and place some of your assets into the trust. These assets are then no longer your assets but the trust's assets. But because you are the trustee in charge of the trust, you still have control over the assets. When you die, if the assets belong to the trust, then the successor trustee that you name in the trust documents automatically gains full control over the assets and distributes them based on what you dictated in the established trust documents.

If you have other assets that are not titled in the trust but belong to you as an individual, then those assets are governed by the will. You can note in your will that you want your assets left to the trust; however, if the assets are valued above the de minimis amount, your heirs now have to go through probate to prove out the will in order to put the assets in the trust to then distribute them subject to the rules of the trust. It would have been much easier to place these assets in the trust in the first place. Now it will take months of probate court and thousands of dollars in lawyer's fees to accomplish the same outcome.

Food for Thought

Place everything you can in the trust except for smaller items that are difficult to title. Things like furniture and family heirlooms should be left to the will because they fall below the de minimis exemption and are difficult to legally place in the trust.

Trust Advantages

The biggest advantage of having a trust is avoiding probate, which can be costly and time consuming. The second advantage to having a trust is that it provides a path for someone else to control your assets if you become incapacitated. If you're still living but are no longer capable of making decisions, a living trust will allow your trustee to take over your affairs. A final advantage of having a trust is that it allows you some amount of control over your assets even *after* your death. For example, a trust will allow you to limit access to your assets if you have a special needs child or very young children. You can dictate in your trust that your children will not have access to your money until a certain time or age.

Trust Details

When it comes to the legal aspects of a trust, there are many complexities that you don't want to overlook. It's important to make sure that after you create the trust you also take the time to title the assets you want in it (this is very important and unfortunately often overlooked). They won't automatically be placed in the trust once you create it. Logistically, this means figuring out what you want included in the trust and then having those items, such as your home, retitled to note that they belong to the trust and not to you.

If you don't have a trust—or at the very least a will—it may be because you want to avoid thinking about death. Unfortunately, none of us can control what the future holds. What we can control is what will happen to the things we have accumulated over the course of our lives. I can know in advance who would benefit from my assets and in what way. Knowing how my belongings can help loved ones I leave behind actually makes it just a little bit easier to face the uncertainty of life.

Many services are available online that can help you get started with the process of writing up a will. If you're looking for something a little more complicated, such as a trust, I highly recommend finding a lawyer who can help you hash out the details. Once you get the "morbid" stuff out of the way, you can enjoy the present with a little less fear of the uncertain future.

CHAPTER 12

Life Insurance

W HILE YOU'RE THINKING about wills and trusts, you may also want to give some thought to life insurance. Having a will or a trust with few assets in them won't do much to protect your family if something happens to you, which is where life insurance can provide a huge lifeline. It's especially important to consider carrying life insurance when you have a young family; if something happens to you, how will your family survive without your income? You may think you don't need life insurance if you're not working outside the home or bringing in the bulk of the family income. But think again; how would your spouse replace what you do now? Without you, your spouse almost certainly would need to start paying for child-care and other services that you take care of now, so having at least a small life insurance policy for yourself is an important decision to consider.

When it comes to purchasing life insurance, many individuals fail to look at the bigger picture. It's common to see people make one-off financial decisions—an insurance policy here, an annuity policy there, another savings account elsewhere—without considering their overall goals. You need to consider whether each of those tools work together or, in some cases, overlap and cancel each other out. It's important that you approach purchasing insurance from a well-informed, eyes-wide-open standpoint.

When to Buy Life Insurance

When it comes to purchasing insurance, I tell my clients to ask themselves three crucial questions:

- What are you insuring for or insuring against?
- How likely is it that a specific negative event will happen?
- What are the consequences if the negative event does happen?

Often, individuals just assume that insurance is important so they go out and buy the first policy they're offered. Insurance *is* important, but purchasing it without fully understanding your situation can lead to a lot of wasted premiums.

A few years back, I let an insurance agent practice his sales pitch on me as a favor to a friend. During the meeting, he tried to convince me that I was in desperate need of life insurance to protect my loved ones. I responded that I had no children and that my husband had equal earning power to myself and would be perfectly fine financially if anything were to happen to me. Not only that, but we had no major debt outside of car payments, and nothing catastrophic would happen to either of us financially if one spouse were to die. Simply put, at that time, my answer to the first crucial question was that there was nothing to insure or insure against, so I had no need for insurance. Now that my husband and I are adding to our family, the situation is different, so we are researching our options to provide for our children if something should happen to us.

We now have something to insure—our child's well-being if she were to lose one or both of her parents.

Now that we've answered the first crucial question, we can move on to the next two: how likely is that negative event (one or both of us passing) and what would be the consequences if it happened?"

The following matrix shows the different combinations of risk frequency and consequences and is helpful in deciding whether or when to buy insurance.

	Consequences Aren't Severe	Consequences Are Severe
Risk Is Infrequent	Do nothing	Insure against risk
Risk Is Frequent	Reduce risk (alter behavior)	Avoid risk (if at all possible)*

You may think it makes the most sense to insure for a frequent risk with severe consequences, but unfortunately most insurance agencies won't insure you for a risk that is frequent because it is too costly for them.

The chance that my spouse or I will die in the near future is low (I'm hoping that it doesn't happen for a very long time), but the consequences are very severe (my child would be left without one or both parents). Thus, we should consider insurance to protect our child against such consequences. Before we had children, if my husband or I died, the financial consequences would not have been severe (my husband and I could have continued to earn enough to maintain a single lifestyle). Knowing that the risk of one of us dying was low and the consequence was mild led me to do nothing.

Let's look at this concept in a common situation that does not involve life or death. Whenever you buy a new gadget, such as a phone, the salesperson often encourages you to buy insurance for the gadget. Let's look at the chart on page 143 to determine if we need that insurance. The risk of me dropping my phone is actually pretty high—I do it all the time. But the consequences are not severe—if the phone becomes unusable, I could buy another one, use an old phone, or simply go without. So, buying expensive insurance to replace my phone if it gets broken is probably not a good financial move. Instead, I should take steps to reduce the risk, such as purchasing a protective case or being more mindful about how I use the phone.

Hopefully, visualizing a chart like this one and asking yourself the three crucial questions listed on page 142 will help you determine the best time to buy insurance.

Term vs. Whole Life Policies

There are two basic types of insurance policies: term and whole life. (There are others, including universal life, but they're less common so we won't tackle them here.) About 99 percent of people should choose term life insurance because it's cheap and straightforward. If you have kids and you're the primary breadwinner, you should consider purchasing term insurance to insure your future income stream. I think it's best to approach life insurance from a worst-case scenario standpoint: how much does my family need to satisfy their basic living expenses without me?

Let's consider the following scenario:
I am a stay-at-home mom with two preschool kids and little work experience, and my husband is a high school teacher who makes about $65,000 per year. Neither my relatives nor my husband's relatives have much in the way of savings. If something

were to happen to my husband, our family would need money from his life insurance policy to provide for our living expenses. If he died, I could probably find a part-time job making around $20,000 a year. To supplement that, we would want a policy that provided roughly $40,000 to $50,000 more a year to satisfy our basic expenses since we don't expect to receive any additional help from relatives. Because we will need to cover those living expenses for another twenty years or so, we would likely want to purchase a life insurance policy for my husband worth at least $1 million.

Now let's consider another scenario:

My husband and I are both working professionals—he's an engineer, and I'm a financial analyst—with two preschool children. We are both highly employable, and either of us could easily provide for our children if something were to happen to the other spouse. Fortunately, we both have parents who are well-off and could also provide for our children's needs if something happened to both of us. However, my husband and I still want to create a base income that would cover our children's living expenses and leave enough money so that they're able to attend college. Because we are fortunate to have several financial safety nets, we need only minimal insurance coverage—just enough to cover our children's basic living and educational expenses on the off chance that none of their grandparents could provide for them. To do this we will purchase life insurance policies for each of us for no more than half a million dollars.

These two scenarios give you a good idea of how to determine how much life insurance you need. But how do you decide whether to buy term or whole life insurance? The benefit of term insurance is that it's inexpensive, particularly if you're young. I can purchase a half a million dollar policy on myself for about $25 per month. The downside is that I can pay for term insurance for many years, but my family will never see any benefit from those payments unless I die.

What about whole life? Whole life insurance, which is sometimes called permanent insurance, is a combination of an investment product and a life insurance product. Insurance agents are often encouraged to sell this type of policy because they make a whole lot more money than when they sell term insurance. Agents will tell you that the benefit of a whole life policy is that it will accrue a cash benefit, meaning you can get some benefit from your money without dying. However, whole life policies are much more expensive than term insurance policies: a half a million dollar whole life policy will probably cost me closer to $350 per month, a large portion of which is fees. In addition, some insurance agents neglect to tell you that the cash benefit will be incredibly expensive for you to access and that the returns are typically much lower than if you invest in a regular, taxable account.

In a few rare instances, a whole life policy makes sense for estate planning purposes. But that typically only applies when you are closer to retirement age and if you have a huge estate. For most people, it makes much more sense to buy a term policy and invest the difference between the cost of that policy and a whole life plan so that you can continue to build savings for retirement or college expenses.

Understand Your If–Thens

Insurance contracts are tricky. Reading the fine print before you buy any insurance policy really is important. Please do not go out and purchase the first insurance product someone offers you. Investigate. Understand what you're getting and exactly what you are paying. One of the things I dislike about insurance products is that they are often full of hidden fees and "if-thens"—conditions that say "if" one thing happens "then" something else happens. But those conditions usually aren't very clear up front. Clarify the if-thens by explicitly asking the selling agent, "If . . . occurs, what happens?" Ask for any and all situations you can think of:

- *If I die, what exactly happens?*
- *If I don't die and the product terminates, what happens?*
- *If I want to increase or decrease the amount of insurance I have at any point, what happens?*

Food for Thought

Often, insurance agents are counting on you to be too confused by the contracts to try to poke holes in what they're selling. Be smart. Be confident. Ask questions. Understand exactly what you're paying up front for the product and on a monthly basis, any penalties you might pay for terminating early or taking money out, and whether there is any cash value to the product. Fees are a huge part of determining a good policy from a bad policy, so know what you're paying.

When it comes to how the policy itself works, understand that an insurance policy is not the same thing as investing in the stock market. An insurance policy is a contract. It's an agreement between you and the insurance agency to receive money in response to a certain event (if I die, then my family gets money). Every now and then I hear stories of insurance agents selling "special/magical investment opportunities" that allow you to get the upside of the market while avoiding the downside. This investment doesn't exist! If it did, we'd all be investing in it and looking like geniuses! You can, however, agree to a contract where you give an insurance agency your money in return for the upside of the market for a fee (and often commission for the salesperson). The insurance agency then takes your money, does a bunch of math, and tries to invest it in such a way that they make enough money to pay themselves and keep their agreement with you and everyone else. They are not, however, investing in a special/magical investment vehicle.

Don't buy an insurance policy without considering the rest of your financial situation. Know how much money you will realistically need in case you or your spouse dies. Determine how much you can reasonably pay for coverage each month. Before you decide to buy a policy that is tied into the stock market, consider whether you have other accounts invested in the market earning market returns; if so, you probably don't want an insurance policy that does the same but at a more expensive rate.

By and large, insurance products are meant to fall on the conservative spectrum—they don't make you rich, but they keep you safe. Do your research when it comes to finding the best policy for your situation and paying the right price for it, and make sure that your insurance policy is aligned with the rest of your financial goals. The best way to make sure that an insurance agent can't sell you something you don't need is to know what you want before you even begin a conversation.

CHAPTER 13

The Lowdown on Mortgages

PURCHASING A NEW HOME can be daunting. It's likely to be one of the largest purchases you will make in your lifetime, and in many ways when you're signing those closing papers, it feels like you are signing your life away. For me, it helps ease my panic to remember that our entire economy is built on transactions just like this one: individuals borrowing and lending allow us to bake a bigger financial pie so that we might each get a slightly larger piece.

Unlike loading up on credit card debt, taking out a mortgage can be a genuinely smart financial decision because of the economic benefits of owning a home. The main one is *appreciation,* and it happens when the value of your home increases over time. Because the debt that you have taken on is being used to purchase something that has the potential to increase in value, it's not nearly as dangerous as taking out debt to buy pizza or a big screen TV—neither of which are likely to appreciate and make you money in the long-run.

What You Need to Know

Unfortunately, just because a mortgage *can be* a good thing doesn't mean a mortgage is *always* a good thing. You can end up with a bad mortgage if you are not careful. To prevent that, we need to have all of our facts and figures straight before we even begin the process. Sometimes women can feel intimidated because they think mortgage brokers and realtors are speaking a language they've never heard before. So, to help you get started, I've compiled a list of mortgage-related vocabulary terms and concepts I believe you should know before you ever open the door of your nearest bank.[34]

Rates and Terms

There are two main types of mortgages. The most common is a *fixed-rate* mortgage. Like the name implies, a fixed-rate mortgage has a stable interest rate that stays the same during the entire term of the loan. If the rate is 3.75 percent, a common rate on a thirty-year mortgage in 2016, then you will pay 3.75 percent interest on the remaining principal of the loan each year for the entire duration of your loan. Most mortgages are written with either a fifteen- or thirty-year term, which means that's how long you have to completely pay off your mortgage. A thirty-year mortgage will have a higher interest rate but lower monthly payments because you have more time to pay it off. Conversely, a fifteen-year mortgage will have a lower interest rate but higher payments.

The other main type of mortgage is what's known as an *adjustable-rate mortgage* or ARM. An ARM will have a fixed rate of interest for the first one to five years and then it will adjust to higher rates at set intervals. This type of mortgage may be ideal for individuals who don't plan on staying in a house for long and will likely sell before the rate adjusts higher. The prospect of a lower initial interest rate—which will come with lower monthly mortgage payments—may be tempting, but the danger in relying on an ARM is that your monthly payments may increase dramatically when your interest rate adjusts. If you're not prepared to pay those higher payments, you may find yourself in hot water financially.

Down Payments and PMI

A *down payment* is the portion of the home's purchase price that you, the buyer, pay out of pocket and up front. Both sellers and lenders prefer large down payments because they demonstrate your financial stability and ability to pay off the loan over the long term. Ideally you want to make a down payment of 20 percent or more to prevent your having to pay *PMI*.

PMI stands for private mortgage insurance, which is essentially additional insurance that you pay to the lender that helps them insure against the possibility that you may default on the loan. For you, the buyer, being forced to pay PMI means you will be paying an additional premium on top of your monthly payment to the bank. After you've paid down your mortgage or the value of your house has risen enough so that the value of your mortgage is less than 80 percent of the value of your home, PMI goes away and you don't have to make those extra payments anymore.

Ratios

A big part of being eligible for a loan has to do with ratios. The two important ones that you should be aware of are *loan-to-value* and *debt-to-income*. Loan-to-value is the percent of your mortgage in relation to the total value of the house.

For simplicity's sake, let's say your home is worth $100,000 and the current balance of your mortgage is $50,000. Your loan-to-value is 50 percent ($50,000/$100,000 = 50 percent). As we mentioned above, if your loan-to-value ratio is greater than 80 percent, you are required to pay PMI, which goes away once your ratio drops below 80 percent. You can achieve a loan-to-value of 80 percent from the get-go by making a down payment of 20 percent when you purchase the house.

The debt-to-income ratio has to do with how lenders measure your ability to pay the monthly mortgage payment. It is calculated by dividing your monthly debt payment, including your new mortgage, by your monthly income. Let's say that each month you make $3,000 in income but have a $250 monthly car payment; your new mortgage will cost $1,250 per month. In this scenario, your debt-to-income ratio will be 50 percent ($1,500/$3,000 = 50 percent). The higher the ratio, the riskier lenders believe you will be as a borrower because you are more likely to have trouble making the payments. Most lenders will set their maximum debt-to-income ratio at somewhere between 40 and 50 percent.

Food for Thought

The size of the mortgage that a lender will give you will be limited by your debt-to-income ratio. Before you decide to start looking at real estate, calculate how much you earn and how much debt you currently hold. Paying off as much debt as you can will help you qualify for a better mortgage.

Titles and Liens

Put simply, the *title* of the property is a document stating who owns it. Once you purchase a home, the title will need to be transferred from the old owner to you so that you can be declared the legal owner of the home. A *lien* is someone else's claim on the property. If you use a mortgage to buy your house, your lender considers your home as collateral against the loan, which means they get to seize the property as theirs if you stop making your payments. When you are buying a house, the bank will require that you also buy title insurance, which insures there are no liens against the property and that you are free and clear to buy it.

Appraisals and Inspections

Before you can purchase a house, the lender will require that you get it *appraised* by a professional to determine how much the home is worth. The bank wants to make sure that it isn't lending you more money than the property is worth. That way, if you default on the loan, the bank will wind up with a property that's roughly worth the amount they loaned to you. Most buyers want to have a home *inspection* to make sure that there are no major problems with the house, such as a faulty foundation or a leaky roof. Having an inspection done by a professional can go a long way in preventing you from purchasing a home with a bunch of hidden problems that could end up costing you a fortune to fix.

Points

When you are getting a mortgage, you may also consider purchasing what are known as *points*. Points are complex, but the basic gist is that you can buy down the interest rate on the loan by paying more up front, which may make sense if you plan on staying in the home for the duration of the loan. When it comes to the cost of getting a loan, it's worth your while to do your homework. Research current mortgage rates and ask whether or not your bank or other lender offers flexibility in how you pay for the underwriting of your mortgage.

Additional Costs

In addition to the cost of appraisals and inspections, taking on a mortgage and closing on a house incur other costs. Collectively, these costs are known as *closing costs* and usually include fees paid to real estate agents, attorneys, lenders, and any other individuals involved in the selling of the home. When it comes to finalizing the mortgage, the main cost you should consider is the cost to actually receive the loan. Your interest rate covers the cost of borrowing the money, but you also have to pay the lender for putting the loan together (and sometimes an application fee simply to start the process). This cost can come in the form of a *loan origination fee* that you pay to the lender, or it can be negotiated into the rate.

As you go through the home buying process, it's important to always ask any questions that come to mind and keep track of the answers. Write them down in a notebook or track them in your phone and make sure to review all of the facts before making a decision. The more you know, the more informed your decision will be and the better off you'll be in the long run.

PART 5

Sunsets and Social Security: Advice for the Later Years

You must not ever stop being whimsical.
And you must not, ever, give anyone else the
responsibility for your life.

—MARY OLIVER, *UPSTREAM*

On the first day of class my senior year of college, a professor asked us to name someone who had been influential in our life. She then made a simple but profound observation that I have carried with me to this day. She said, "Look for people who have lived a long life and are still happy, because they have something to teach you." Partly because of that piece of advice, I find myself looking for older people who have survived hardships but are still joyful. Contrary to most people in our current culture, I think that age is stunning. Much like the refinement of silver or gold, I believe that aging—and surviving the hardships that tend to accompany a long life—makes us significantly more beautiful.

Since starting out in the field of financial planning, I have heard hundreds of stories and built just as many retirement plans for individuals from a variety of backgrounds. In observing so many different approaches to retirement, one of the things I have learned is that attitude plays a huge role in whether a person views retirement positively. We can't control everything that happens to us, but we can control how we respond to what happens to us. That's what this section is about.

We'll begin by discussing the obstacles to saving for retirement—especially those that affect women—and exploring some of the things you should consider before you decide to retire. After that we'll talk about Social Security—how it works and what you should know before filing to receive your benefits.

Next we'll turn to health care and why you should include health-care expenses in any retirement plan. Then we'll change pace and talk about overcoming some of life's most difficult situations—things like divorce and being widowed—and appreciating some of life's greatest blessings—good friends. Finally, we'll dig into long-term care, and I'll share some tips on financial steps you can take to prepare for the unexpected.

CHAPTER 14

Saving for Retirement Is Hard

EARLY IN 2016, the Consumer Federation of America released its ninth annual *America Saves Week* survey in which it polled roughly 1,000 nonretired Americans regarding their readiness to retire.[35] As in previous years, the 2016 survey found that the majority of Americans were insufficiently prepared for retirement, leading the organization to note that only 40 percent of respondents felt they were making "good or excellent progress in 'meeting their savings needs.'" Additionally, while roughly half of participants said they were saving at least 5 percent of their income, only 43 percent were saving outside of work and only 38 percent reported having no consumer debt.

While these statistics are sobering enough, even more concerning is the gender gap revealed by the survey. While 74 percent of men reported making progress with their savings, only 67 percent of women could say the same. About 72 percent of men reported spending less than they earned and saving the difference, but only 60 percent of women were doing the same. According to that survey, 40 percent of American women are digging themselves into a black hole of debt, compared to only 28 percent of men!

When looking at these statistics, it's easy to lay the blame on income inequality or the lack of feminists on the battle-field. But in truth, like most complex economic issues, many variables play into these numbers. For starters, women have long fulfilled the role of caregivers, which has historically meant stepping back from the workforce to care for children or aging parents and grandparents. My mother has been both a stay-at-home mom and a caregiver for my late grandmother, and she did an excellent job at both. I have personally chosen to pursue a working-girl lifestyle, but that doesn't make me any less thankful that my mom made the choices she did. One consequence of her decision is that my mom has had significantly fewer opportunities to save for retirement than my dad did. Thus, the bulk of my parent's retirement savings is under my dad's name. My parents have a strong marriage, and both expect that my dad's retirement nest egg will be shared between them.

However, not every couple has this expectation of a shared retirement fund, and knowing that most of your savings are listed under your spouse's name may be cause for concern. Depending on the laws in the state where you reside, you are usually entitled to receive a portion of your spouse's retirement assets should your marriage dissolve. While no one enters a marriage hoping it will end, it's still a good idea to have a basic knowledge of your spouse's assets so that you can know what to expect and avoid being taken advantage of. Sadly, dividing the assets when a marriage ends may leave both parties significantly underprepared for retirement. Additionally, women who find themselves on their own financially soon realize that the majority of financial wisdom is written by and for men. Women make up 50 percent of our workforce—whether they are working in an office or working in the home—and they deserve to be valued a little better by the financial sector. I cannot close all the wage and respect gaps, but I do hope this little book can at least help a few women take control of their own financial future.

Saving When You're Behind

Saving is hard work, especially if you're a woman. While there are plenty of acceptable reasons for falling behind, that doesn't change the fact that you may have some catching up to do in order to make your financial goals a reality. If you're behind, don't lose hope. You owe it to yourself to put on some brightly colored lipstick, lift your head high, and bravely face the task that lies ahead: catching up.

If it's time for you to start catching up, then it's also time to make some changes. This is the hardest part. Change is hard. Cutting back on your spending isn't fun, but if the financial goal of an adequate retirement fund is important to you, then it's something that needs to happen—and soon. The longer you put it off, the harder it's going to be and truthfully, you may run out of time to make it happen. Luckily, you can do a few things to be more efficient with your savings that should make the process of catching up a little less painful.

Max Out Your Retirement Savings

If your employer offers a 401(k) or 403(b) savings option, the best place to start your savings catch-up is by maxing out your contributions. At the very least, contribute enough to receive the maximum matching contribution from your employer because that is free extra money to you. If you can handle the hit to your spending, make an effort to contribute the maximum amount. The IRS has made it beneficial for you to do this by allowing you to deduct your contributions at tax time, which also saves you money in the present.

The first deduction from your paycheck for your retirement account will be the hardest because you will miss it from your budget the most. But over time you will miss that money less and less as you get used to living without it. In the meantime, your retirement account will begin to grow, and before you know it, you will have accumulated a substantial amount. If your employer doesn't offer any type of retirement benefit, set up an IRA and contribute the maximum amount on your own. (See information in chapter 6 for further details about retirement accounts and how best to contribute to them. While the information is about 401(k)s, as opposed to IRAs, the traditional vs. Roth discussion is still relevant.)

Start Small and Work Your Way Up

If maxing out your retirement contributions sounds unthinkable to you because you do not have that much flexibility in your budget, then start small. Contribute enough to earn the match from your employer. Then slowly increase your contribution. Start by contributing 5 percent of your gross salary a month, and every few months increase your contribution by another 1 percent.

By starting small and making small increases, you can slowly ease yourself into a change in your savings status. Contribute enough of each paycheck to your retirement account or IRA so that you feel a *little* pain. When it's no longer painful to live without that chunk of change, add a little more to your monthly contribution. The key here is that you will be making progress, even if it doesn't feel like it at the beginning.

Contribute Bonuses

If you're not yet ready to face a regular change in spending, commit to contributing any bonuses you receive towards retirement savings. Hopefully, because bonuses aren't guaranteed, you don't rely on them for your day-to-day living expenses. If you do, stop it right now! You should never build your lifestyle on income that isn't steady and somewhat guaranteed.

Committing your bonuses or any other irregular earning to retirement savings is a great way to kick-start your savings habit. Even if you're already saving extra from your paychecks each month, you may still want to consider saving from your bonus. Personally, I like to split my bonuses between savings and treats for myself. That way I can enjoy the fruits of my reward while still feeling like I'm being a responsible adult.

Commit to Saving in the Future

If the previous options all seem completely out of range for you, commit to start saving in the future. You can do this by setting up all future raises to go to your retirement savings account. That may sound cruel and unfair, but remember: you're behind. If you want to catch up, something needs to change. If you cannot or you're not willing to change your situation now, you can commit to holding your living standards at their current level and letting future additional income go toward catching you up on the savings front.

Some companies even have options to let you automatically contribute future raises to your 401(k). By setting up your raises to automatically go into savings, you won't even know they're missing because you never saw them drop into your checking account in the first place.

Food for Thought

If you're not sure whether or not you're on track with your retirement savings, it may be time to meet with a financial advisor to discuss your goals and current savings. A good advisor will be able to match the two together and give you a good idea of whether or not you're on track to meet your goals.

How Much Is Needed?

A lot goes into deciding whether you're saving enough for retirement. Some of the factors, such as your savings rate, how early you start, and how long you work, are easier to know. Others, such as how long you'll live and what the state of the market will be when you retire are impossible to nail down. All of these different inputs complicate the question, "Am I saving enough?"

For simplicity's sake, we've created a chart based on research by respected retirement expert Wade Pfau. The table shows what multiple of your current income you should have saved based on how old you are and what percent of your income you expect to save each year for the rest of your working years.

How Much You Should Have
Saved Up to Retire at 65

Current Age	If You're Saving 5%*	If You're Saving 10%*	If You're Saving15%*
At Age 35	2x current income	1x current income	0x current income
At Age 45	4x current income	3x current income	2x current income
At Age 50	6x current income	5x current income	4x current income
At Age 60	10x current income	10x current income	10x current income

*of your income for the remainder of your working life.
Source: W. Pfau, "Getting on Track for Retirement."

For example: Consider a forty-five-year old who plans on saving 5 percent of what she makes each year for the rest of her working years. She should have four times her current salary saved up. If she makes $100,000 each year, then she should have $400,000 currently saved (4 × $100,000 = $400,000) for retirement if she hopes to retire at age sixty-five. By the time she's sixty, she should have ten times her income, which would be $1 million (10 × $100,000).

For someone who hopes to retire earlier, as you can probably imagine, more should be saved. You may have also noticed that the numbers in the chart converge the closer one gets to retirement, and that by the time you're 60 (retirement age) the amount you need to have saved is the same regardless of how much you're saving. This is because the closer you get to retiring, the less time you have left to save. These last years are also prime years for earning more on your investments because your overall savings pot is at its largest. It's also important to note that the closer you are to retirement, the less helpful general rules-of-thumb are.

It's always a good idea to look into building a financial plan based on your actual savings and needs at least five years prior to your anticipated retirement date to make sure you really are on track.

CHAPTER 15

Time to Retire?

T HE FIRST STEP in retiring is figuring out whether you can—if you have enough money to live on for the rest of your life. This is the most important step because if you mess it up, your retirement is in danger. If you retire too early, there's a chance you could run out of money, and it's incredibly difficult for ex-retirees to find a job these days. Once you decide to retire, your employer isn't going to hold your spot in case you change your mind, so you had better be pretty certain of your decision.

If you think you're ready to retire, the very best thing you can do is have your financial plan updated, preferably by a certified financial planner—someone who lists "CFP®" after their name on their letterhead. To learn more about the CFP® designation, check out Appendix B. Or you can just trust me when I say that CFP®s are respected individuals in the financial planning industry and are more likely to provide you with a good financial plan.

Factors to Consider
When reviewing your retirement plan, you'll want to make sure that it takes into account all of the following factors.

Inflation

Over time, things cost more because of what's known as inflation. If you don't believe me, consider this: in 1986 a Big Mac cost $1.60. Today it costs $4.79.[36] You will need more to live off of in the future than you need now, so make sure your retirement plan includes a cost-of-living adjustment to help you keep up with inflation.

Health Care

Although your employer probably offered you health-care benefits while you were working, it's much less likely they'll continue to offer those same benefits after you retire. In fact, you'll be one of the lucky ones if they offer any benefits at all. But you still need health insurance, which means you'll need to pay for it on your own.

Depending on when you choose to retire, you may also have to bridge the gap from working until you're old enough to receive Medicare, which will cover most but not all of your health-care expenses. For this reason, it's important that your financial plan includes expenditures for health care.

Wiggle Room

It's safe to assume that the future is uncertain. So you don't want to retire based on a plan that allows you just enough money to squeak by. You want to leave a margin of error for uncertainties.

What if the financial markets take a hit right after you retire? Does your plan leave room for that? What if you decide to travel or undertake a major remodeling project at home? Is there extra room in your plan for extra spending? You don't know how your retirement will play out, so do yourself a favor and try not to cut it too close. It's much better to wind up with a little left over than to run out of money while your body and mind are still going strong.

Talking Logistics

Once you know you have a plan that will allow you to retire comfortably, the next step is letting your employer know when you plan to retire. "Of course I need to let my employer know," you say. It does feel like a bit of a *duh* statement, but I want to remind you that your boss needs to hear the news from you—not from friends you've told about your plans.

Having to replace an employee while keeping an organization running smoothly is one of any company's biggest challenges, so be respectful and transparent with your employer. Give plenty of notice and do your best to help with the transition. It will reflect positively on you and make your employer much more willing to help you receive your retirement benefits in a timely manner.

Move Money Wisely

Now that you've let everybody know your good news, it's time to focus on the logistics of tapping into that money you've been saving all these years. As long as your money is in your 401(k) it maintains what is known as *qualified* tax status, meaning it receives tax-friendly treatment. The second you withdraw that money, it ceases to be qualified and becomes taxable. This means that if you cash out your 401(k) all at once and deposit that check at your local bank you will be nailed with a huge tax bill because you will be taxed on the entire balance of your 401(k) as if it were income. Don't do that. Instead, open an IRA and roll over the money. IRAs are also qualified accounts and as long as your money moves from one qualified account to another, it retains its tax-friendly status.

Food for Thought

If you are lucky enough to retire before you turn fifty-nine and one-half, you need to be very careful about how you fund your retirement. The IRS will hit you with a 10 percent penalty for pulling money out of your qualified accounts before you turn 59.5. If you are looking to retire before that age, you need to have an ample amount of cash available to bridge the gap. If you don't, the IRS will allow some workarounds, but they have to be executed flawlessly or the IRS will hit you with that 10 percent penalty and make you pay it going backward, which is no fun. If you choose to go this route, make sure you find someone who is an expert in these workarounds and can make sure that everything goes according to the letter of the law.

Once you have your new accounts set up and your money rolled over, you're ready to retire! Simply walk out of your office and start golfing. Or bird watching. Or hanging out with your grandkids. Or whatever it is you want to do. Enjoy the rest and relaxation. You've earned it!

Every now and then, you should check in with your financial advisor to make sure that you're adhering to your plan and not depleting your assets too quickly. Ideally, you want the earnings on your savings (in addition to proceeds from things like annuities, pensions, and social security) to help cover your spending needs. As long as your accounts are holding steady or increasing, you're in good shape. If you find that you're spending them down, you may need to reevaluate your retirement lifestyle and consider cutting back on your spending to avoid running out of money.

CHAPTER 16

Everything You Need to Know about Social Security

AS A FINANCIAL ADVISOR at a time when baby boomers are retiring in droves, I know all too well how important Social Security is to the success of most retirement plans. Although there are concerns about the long-term viability of the Social Security system, most financial experts believe it will continue to exist as a major financial pillar for retirees, even if some benefits are reduced or terms are changed. However, women already face some disadvantages in the Social Security system, which you need to understand.

As I wrote in chapter 14, one of the primary reasons many women have less saved for retirement is because they earn less and are more likely to leave the workforce for periods of time to take care of children or ailing relatives. This pattern also has a negative consequence on women's Social Security benefits. To be eligible for Social Security retirement benefits, individuals need to earn a total of forty credits during their working life. You earn four credits for each year you work and pay Social Security taxes, so you must work and pay into the system for at least ten years to be eligible for your own retirement benefits.

Food for Thought

Because more individuals are currently or may soon be taking from the Social Security system than are paying into it, the Social Security trust fund could be depleted in the next twenty years at current usage rates. It's important to understand what this means before you freak out. Even if the fund is depleted, it would not mean that Social Security benefits would go away entirely. The working population will continue to pay into Social Security; however, it could mean that people receiving Social Security will get less than the full benefit they have been expecting. The U.S. government could take many different steps in the next few years to increase revenue or reduce benefits in order to bridge the gap. Pay attention to any program modifications that are proposed and to how they will affect your retirement plans.

Additionally, the size of your retirement benefit is determined in part by an average of your income. For most people, the longer they work, the more likely their income is to rise as they are promoted or take new, higher-paying positions. Women who leave the workforce for even a few years may never catch up to the earnings of their male colleagues. The combination of fewer years in the workplace and lower lifetime earnings results in smaller Social Security retirement benefits for women. A recent article in *Time* noted the unfortunate consequences:

In 2013, the poverty rate for single—never married, divorced and widowed—women age 65 and older was nearly three times what it was for married women. The poverty rate for white, single women age 65 and older now stands at almost 1 in 6, according to 2013 census data. For African-American women it's 1 in 3, and for Hispanic women it's nearing 1 in 2.[37]

While I wouldn't go so far as to blame women's poverty rates on Social Security alone, I have no doubt that the formula for distributing retirement benefits plays a role because I know that Social Security makes up a significant portion of retirement income for most individuals. Keep this issue in mind during future elections and legislative discussions about Social Security.

Key Social Security Provisions

Women should be aware of several Social Security provisions when they are planning for retirement. Understanding these issues can help you make choices that could affect your life for years to come.

Spousal Benefits

In 1939, the Social Security Administration changed the way benefits are structured to better provide for families and not just individuals.[38] As a result, spouses are able to receive up to 50 percent of the higher-earning-spouse's retirement benefit. This provision helps reduce some of the negative impact to women's benefits that was discussed earlier.

If you have earned the forty credits necessary to become eligible for your own retirement benefit, you can choose to take your earned benefit or the spousal benefit—whichever is higher. If your spouse earned far more than you did over your careers, you will likely be better off taking the spousal benefit; if your earnings have been near the same level, you will probably be better off taking your own.

If you are divorced after being married for at least ten years, you are still eligible to receive 50 percent of your ex-spouse's benefit—whether or not your ex remarries. However, you cease to be eligible for that spousal option from your ex if *you* remarry.

Survivor's Benefits

Should your spouse pass away, you become eligible to receive 100 percent of their benefit (if it's higher than your current benefit). As a survivor, you can begin receiving your spouse's benefits as early as age sixty, but you will receive a reduced amount by filing early.[39] If you want to receive 100 percent of their benefit, you'll need to wait until you've reached full retirement age (sixty-six or sixty-seven depending on when you were born). If you are eligible for your own benefit, you may want to consider taking your spousal benefit, even if it is lower, and delay switching to your benefit until a later age, allowing it to grow in the meantime. If you have a child who is a minor at the time of your spouse's passing, you may be eligible to receive spousal benefits early and your child may also be eligible to receive a survivor benefit.

This benefit also applies to ex-spouses as well. If your ex-spouse dies, you're still eligible to receive 100 percent of that benefit. The same exception rules that apply to spousal benefits also apply to survivors benefits: you must have been married at least ten years and cannot have remarried. Social Security is a complex topic with a variety of strategies that you can pursue. If you become a widow, you should first call the Social Security office to understand your benefits and learn how to begin receiving them (you'll need to collect several important documents such as birth, marriage, and death certificates). Before filing, you may also want to contact a financial planning expert to discuss the various strategies available to you to give you a better chance of choosing the best strategy for your specific situation.

Timing Is Important

Whether you're receiving your own or spousal benefits, plan carefully before you file to start receiving payments. Depending on when you were born, full retirement age is considered to be sixty-six or sixty-seven. Although you can start receiving Social Security benefits starting as early as age sixty-two, you will be penalized for taking the early retirement option. On the other hand, you get a bonus if you delay your retirement, with the amount rising by a few percentage points for every year you delay up to age seventy.

Just like with your personal Social Security benefits, if you file early for spousal benefits, you will receive less. This means that if you file at sixty-two, you will receive closer to 35 percent of your spouse's benefit as opposed to 50 percent, and it won't bump up to 50 percent when you reach full retirement age.

Food for Thought

Take time to understand the various Social Security benefits that you will receive by filing before, at, or after your full retirement age. Make sure you understand exactly what you will be getting and all the relevant trade-offs. Women who are eager to receive additional income often make the mistake of filing early for their Social Security benefits and, as a result, end up receiving significantly less over the course of their retirement. This may be another factor contributing to women's overall lower levels of Social Security benefits.

The Skinny on Health Care in Retirement

If you haven't heard the news already, women are living longer than men. Depending on who you ask, we're living longer than our male counterparts by anywhere from three to ten years. This is probably because we are so awesome. Unfortunately, it also means greater health-care expenditures for us in retirement.

According to a study by Professor Allison Hoffman of the UCLA School of Law and Professor Howell Jackson of Harvard Law School, we're also underestimating by quite a bit how much we'll need in order to pay for health care.[40] Hoffman and Jackson asked 1,700 individuals close to retirement to estimate what they expected to pay out of pocket for health expenses. The estimates from women were 50 percent lower than the estimates from men despite the fact that women will likely end up paying more. According to HealthView Services, women can expect to pay roughly $208,266 over the course of their retirement for Medicare parts B, D, supplemental premiums, and cost sharing, compared to $186,688 for men.[41]

Ultimately, your costs will be determined by your level of income in retirement and the type of insurance you use. For some retirees, corporate retirement plans from previous employers will help fill the gap of expensive health-care costs; however, these types of benefits are becoming less and less common. If you don't anticipate receiving health-care benefits from a previous employer, it is worth your while to spend some time researching what you might expect to pay out of pocket in retirement. One great resource is the Medicare website (medicare.gov). You can also go to your state's health insurance website to get an estimate of what different insurers offer based on where you live.

Whatever you do, make sure you do *something*. Health care is a significant portion of spending at any age, and it's important not to underestimate the impact it will have on your retirement.

CHAPTER 17

Bunco and Best Friends

M Y MOTHER IS CONSTANTLY throwing parties. Party throwing is her superpower. All my life, she has been gathering people into her home and feeding them. From block parties to bridal showers to tea parties—she does it all. Thursdays are bunco days with the ladies. I happened to be writing this chapter one Thursday, and I chose to work at my mom's kitchen counter. I couldn't help myself. I wanted to be near this group of women.

My mother is the youngest and, surprisingly, the tamest in this group of roughly fifteen women who take turns hosting their weekly games. They are loud. They shout when they win and bang their hands on the table when they lose; every ten minutes someone is accused of cheating. Their time together is pure, unadulterated joy, and the joy that I feel watching them is enriched because I know bits and pieces of their stories.

The longer you live, the greater your chances are of experiencing truly wonderful things and horribly painful things, and these women have experienced both. In the course of one morning's conversation, they discuss the wedding of one and the chemo of another. They have weathered many trials of life, and yet here they are—popping jelly beans like there's no tomorrow and drinking raspberry lemonade from clear plastic cups designed to look like fancy crystal. They make me deep-belly laugh. They are stunning.

Friendship and Grace

In a lot of ways, my mom's bunco buddies remind me of my best friend, who I met my sophomore year of college while we were both studying in Italy. Her name is Grace. It is the first thing she tells anyone new: "Hi! I'm Grace!" I could not stand Grace for the first four months we were living together in our study-abroad program. Grace is loud and bright. I am introverted and like neutral colors. Grace deals with conflict up front. I am the queen of passive aggression. Grace spent our year abroad growing out her leg hairs while I washed and folded laundry for the both of us. Grace is at odds with all of the ways that I believe I am perfect. We are unlikely friends to say the least.

A few years into our friendship, Grace stood next to me the night my mom called to tell me about my grandma's cancer, waiting to catch me when my insides broke and the tears came. When there were no tears left, we borrowed her boyfriend's truck and drove to the nearest grocery store to buy Graeter's Black Raspberry Chocolate Chip Ice Cream. Graeter's ice cream is one of my favorites—rich and creamy, thick with real milk and actual berries. The chocolate chips are less "chips" and more like giant hunks of fudge that melt and slide down your throat as soon as they hit your tongue.

In the months since we had returned from Italy, Black Raspberry Chocolate Chip had become our "tragedy ice cream." We ate it over failed tests and internship rejections.

We ate it when we were angry and cramping. We ate it to mourn change and to take a break from all of the chaos of growing up.

That night, Grace and I drove back to my apartment in silence while I cradled that pint of escape. I was living in a ramshackle apartment complex with not nearly enough parking for all of the college students who had managed to cram themselves in. The paved spots out front were all taken, but we felt invincible enough to take on the dirt lot since we were in a truck. I jumped out to help with the parking; I could see that Grace needed to maneuver the pickup over a slab of concrete, but there was plenty of space and only a bit of foliage in front of her. I gave Grace the go-ahead and she hit the gas, barreling over that slab of concrete and straight into a metal rod hiding in the foliage. As we heard the loud crunch of the bumper, our eyes locked—horrified.

I stared at the ground while Grace shared the unfortunate news with the truck's owner. We made our way to my room, plopped down on my bed, and burst out laughing. That night we ate the entire pint of "tragedy ice cream."

I owe a great deal of my growing up to Grace. Without Grace, I am this little, bitter ball of fury. Grace made me soft. She taught me that it was OK to feel things deep down and be vulnerable with others. It is because of Grace that I met my husband Tom, and it was Grace who stood next to me when I married him. It was Grace's shoulder that I cried on the morning my precious grandma passed away, and it is Grace's number that I dial when I hurt and need to tell someone. I love Grace in a way that I love no one else—different from the way that I love my husband and my parents, different from the way that I love my daughter.

Weaving Friendships

We live in a world that claims to offer immense potential for connection, but it's not enough to have 5,000 Facebook friends. We need tangible, reach-out-and-poke-each-other, honest-to-goodness friends. True friends like Grace and like the women in my mom's bunco group make life worth living. We don't get to choose our family, but our friends are the family that life chooses for us. They start out as strangers then slowly weave the threads of their story into our own.

We need good friends. Women especially need friends, as has been proven in study after study—and in our life experiences. As women, we face so many difficulties. Battles with our looks and our bodies, insecurities, lost relationships, miscarriages, cancer, caring for ailing parents, and the list goes on. Life is hard. It's deliciously wonderful and at times bursting with so much joy, but it is also hard. The next few chapters are about the hard times—the times when we most need our best friends.

If you are currently down there in the mud and it feels like everything is falling apart, I hope you have a friend to reach for. One who is willing to bend down and help pull you out, or maybe even just sit there with you, feeling your pain and being willing to share your burden. If you are currently in a season of great joy, I hope you are surrounding yourself with dear friends who can join in your celebration.

Most of all, whether you are in the mud or on the mountaintop without a best friend to share your experience, I hope you will consider opening yourself up to someone who has the potential to become one. Good friends aren't established overnight. It takes many nights, many phone calls, many games of bunco, many pints of tragedy ice cream and accidental fender benders, tears of laughter and tears of deep heartache to build a strong friendship. But I am absolutely convinced that having truly close friends is one of life's greatest treasures, and as you'll see in the next few chapters, friends can even make it a little easier to deal with some of life's greatest financial upheavals.

CHAPTER 18

Overcoming the Hard Stuff

SOMETIMES, THINGS HAPPEN that you have no way of preparing for. The spring before my wedding, on a very memorable Easter morning, I discovered a terrifying little lump that subsequently required multiple doctor's visits and eventually had to be surgically removed. Luckily, the lump turned out to be benign, but in the in-between I lost many nights of sleep worrying about my suddenly uncertain future.

I am a worrier. Over the years I have made numerous spreadsheets in feeble attempts to solve my fear of uncertainty. My parents have gray hairs that are undoubtedly the result of late-night phone calls from their anxious daughter. I can't help myself. I want to be in control. I want to define what happens. Unfortunately, the truth of the matter is that I can't. I have no clue where this life will take me.

So much of life is determined by our attitudes and how we respond to the circumstances life presents us rather than the nature of our circumstances. We all have our battles. It seems I can't go a day without hearing of some painful circumstances that tear at my heart—a friend's divorce, a neighbor's miscarriage, a colleague's illness. Even minor life struggles can be hard when you're in the middle of them. I have learned that we can't escape trouble, and we can't change how we feel, but we can change how we respond.

Life is messy, and there is no way you can ever prepare for every contingency. However, you can take steps to help prevent a difficult event from wiping you out financially. The last thing you want in times of crisis is to be worrying about money. Taking time to plan for the worst isn't inviting trouble—it's giving you a lifeline to hold onto when trouble strikes.

Overcoming Divorce

I want to be up front and admit I am not qualified to write about this topic in a general way. I have had no first-hand or even second-hand knowledge of divorce. As a financial advisor, however, I have seen the effects of divorce and how difficult and painful it can be. In addition to the burden of splitting up assets and debt—trying to decide who gets what and who's responsible for what—the emotional toll can be so great that it impairs judgment.

I want to approach this topic as sensitively as possible while still offering advice that can be helpful. My hope is that if you ever find yourself in this process, you can find financial advisors who will be helpful and also sensitive. You should not be expected to have everything together in such an emotional time, but do take some proactive steps to take care of yourself and your financial well-being.[42]

Avoid Doing Anything Rash

Depending on the nature of your divorce, you may find yourself wanting to go on a crazy spending spree to get back at your spouse or to feel better about yourself. As much fun as this may feel in the short run, it's a bad idea in the long run. You both have legal responsibilities to avoid actions that will harm the other party in regard to your joint assets. Always keep that in mind when making financial decisions at this stage.

Likewise, the courts look unfavorably upon any party who attempts to get sneaky and hide assets. Do yourself a favor and leave everything out in the open. Avoid all appearances of mishandling your joint accounts, and keep careful records of anything you're spending. You want to be able to prove you haven't done anything to harm the other party if any such accusations are made later.

Consider Your Future Circumstances

When I first shared my desire to write this book, a dear family friend left me a long voicemail message saying it was imperative that I warn women in the midst of a divorce to ask about who will pay for their children's future college costs. This is my ode to her voicemail.

This may be a difficult and challenging time, and you may be trying to get through it as quickly and with as little conflict as possible. But the decisions you make now have long-term consequences, and you need to take the time to consider what some of those long-term consequences might be. My friend focused only on what she and her children needed in the short-term. No one advised her that she should ask what would happen ten years later when her youngest child would be ready for college. Because she didn't ask, the issue of who would pay for college was not included in the divorce settlement, and she ended up shouldering a much bigger financial burden than she expected.

Close Your Joint Accounts

It helps keep everyone honest if you begin the process of splitting your joint accounts as soon as a divorce looks likely. In most divorce situations, half of the assets belong to each of you, so you don't need to wait for a final settlement to divide your joint accounts. If you take more than half of any account, you will probably have to replace that money later on, so don't bother trying. Save yourself that hassle and split it down the middle from the get-go.

Also try to close out joint credit card accounts to prevent either party from maxing them out. You may have to consult an attorney first if you're carrying a large amount of debt on the cards because that can make the process much trickier. But if possible, pay off the debt, cancel the cards, and apply for new ones individually.

Pay Off Debt

When you sit down to split up your assets, go ahead and split up the debt as well. This can become messy quickly because creditors would rather not transfer all of the debt to one spouse. It's better for them to hold both of you accountable. Thus, the easiest way to get rid of the debt is to pay it off in equal parts. If you are financially unable, an alternative may be to refinance the debt as individuals. You should be very wary of maintaining debt that includes both of your names on it because you could be left holding the whole bag if your ex chooses not to pay their share.

Consider Hiring an Attorney or Mediator

Contrary to how divorce attorneys are presented on TV, they are usually sensitive and helpful in real life. Having one to function as a mediator can be incredibly helpful since they are immune to the emotional aspects that are keeping you from making good decisions. Hiring an attorney or mediator doesn't necessarily mean you expect to have a major conflict with your soon-to-be-ex. It is just a step that can reduce stress, which is better for everyone in the long run.

Be Flexible

Make an inventory of all of your joint assets, debt, and income so that you can initiate a rational conversation about how everything will be split. Know that a contested divorce can be very costly, so it's in everyone's best interest to come to a mutual agreement. Be flexible when negotiating so that you can focus on the issues that matter to you most.

Overcoming Being Widowed

If you are a recent widow or someone who has endured widowhood for a long time, I want to start by saying that I cannot begin to fathom where you're at or what you're feeling or have felt in the past. But please know that I ache for you, no matter what circumstances brought you to this point. Shortly after her husband died in a freak accident, Sheryl Sandberg, COO of Facebook, wrote about dealing with her grief and finding ways to move forward in what I found to be one of the most painful and yet strikingly beautiful pieces of writing I have ever read:

I was talking to one of these friends about a father-child activity that Dave is not here to do. We came up with a plan to fill in for Dave. I cried to him, "But I want Dave. I want option A." He put his arm around me and said, "Option A is not available. So let's just kick the **** out of option B."[43]

Sandberg ends her letter by saying that she will always mourn for option A but that she promises to do all she can to make the most of what she has left. That is what this chapter is about—doing the best you can with what you've been left with.

As I've worked with women who have been widowed, I have noticed that one of the greatest advantages they can have, particularly when it comes to figuring out finances, is a friend or family member who is willing to walk alongside them through the process. When a spouse dies, the list of issues the survivor must deal with is often overwhelming, especially because the tasks arise in the midst of so many emotions. So my first word of advice to a new widow is to find at least one person you know you can trust, ask for their help, and then heavily lean on them during this time. There is no shame in depending on others for support, particularly during a difficult time.

Next, with the help of your support person, begin to collect information. Find out who is in charge of your late spouse's various financial accounts and contact them. When a person dies, their accounts go through a period of "limbo" while financial personnel try to figure out who now owns the accounts and what their wishes are. You can help shorten this "in-between" period by getting organized and reaching out to each of those entities. Let them know what you know and then let them do their work. They should be able to tell you if there's anything urgent that needs to be taken care of right away. If nothing is urgent, it's perfectly fine to say you'll get back in touch later. When you're ready, here are some of the issues you'll need to tackle.

Your Spouse's Retirement Pension

If your spouse had a pension, you may be eligible to receive a portion of the payments, depending on how the pension plan was set up. This is true if your spouse elected to have pension payments reduced in exchange for the guarantee that a portion of the pension would continue to be paid to a surviving spouse. In order to find out, you should call the Human Resources office at your spouse's former employer and ask if you're eligible. If you are, then determine the necessary steps to transfer the pension payments to your name.

Your Spouse's IRA

If your spouse left behind an IRA and named you as the beneficiary, you'll need to set up a new account and roll over the funds. As a spouse, you get special treatment when it comes to inheriting an IRA, which affects whether or not you have to take required minimum distributions (RMDs) on the account. Unlike other IRA beneficiaries, you have the option of rolling over an inherited IRA into an IRA under your name. This option allows you to delay RMDs if you are under the age of seventy and one-half. If you are older than fifty-nine and one-half this is typically your best bet. If you are not yet fifty-nine and one-half it is typically better to transfer the assets to an inherited IRA in the name of your deceased spouse because it allows you to access the money without penalties, which you wouldn't have been able to do otherwise; however, you will need to pay the RMDs if you choose this option. How much you're required to withdraw is based on your spouse's age at death, your current age, and the balance of the account on December 31 of the year they passed. Hold onto any financial statements you've received for this account in case they're needed to help calculate the RMD.

Your Spouse's Social Security

Once your spouse dies, you become eligible to receive survivors Social Security benefits based on your spouse's benefit. Just like your regular benefit, your survivors benefit is also reduced for each additional year that you choose to take it early prior to full retirement age. For example, if you choose to take your survivor's benefit at age sixty, the total amount you receive will be reduced by about 30 percent. If you are eligible to receive your own benefit, you have the option of starting your own benefit at age sixty-two and then switching to 100 percent of your survivor's benefit at full retirement age if it is higher than your benefit. To receive your spouse's benefit, contact the Social Security office and let them know you'd like to start receiving your deceased spouse's benefit. They can let you know what steps you need to take to begin those payments. One of the biggest mistakes a widow can make is taking this benefit too early. With that in mind, it might be a good idea to consult a financial planner who can help you maximize your benefits.

Other Accounts

If your spouse left behind other accounts that were solely in their name, you'll need to retitle those accounts under your name—assuming you are the sole beneficiary of those accounts. It may be helpful at this time to consolidate some accounts. A financial advisor should be able to help you with this process.

Overcoming Long-Term Care Issues

I know that not everyone can provide in-home care for their elderly relatives, and not everyone will have the chance to die at home. It's messy and complicated and sometimes you just need help. But I have watched both my mother and her mother care for their mothers-in-law, and I can honestly say it's one of the most beautiful things I have ever witnessed. There is something truly precious about caring for someone's physical needs, providing them dignity and allowing them to gracefully pass through the twilight of life.

Caring for my grandmother was really, really hard for my mom. Fortunately for everyone, hospice caregivers came to take care of the messiest stuff, but the process still took a heavy emotional toll on my mom, even though she has some fond memories from those years. As a daughter and a new mother, I can say that watching my mom from afar has given me a deep respect for what she did and who she is, and I hope I will be able to offer such loving care to her and my mother-in-law when the time comes.

It took me a long time to write this section, largely because I didn't know where to start. Long-term care is a very complicated topic because it is so expensive and because there is simply no great way to approach it. Unfortunately, it's also a very real need. In 2000, nearly 10 million people in the U.S. required some form of long-term care, and more than 60 percent of them were over the age of sixty-five. Almost 70 percent of people now turning sixty-five will need long-term care at some point in their lives.[44]

When my grandmother found out she had cancer, she said she didn't want any treatment and would gladly move into a nursing home of some sort. My mother wouldn't hear of it and insisted that my grandmother move in with my parents and younger brother. It was agreed that a hospice team would provide assistance with Grandma's daily living activities such as bathing, dressing, and using the toilet. This type of long-term care, which may also include activities like housecleaning, shopping, and food preparation, is less likely to be covered by health insurance because it is not considered medical care. These activities are important elements of day-to-day life that we rarely think about, but we often need help with them as we age.

Although the amount of long-term care varies with each individual, women tend to need more long-term care than men because they typically live longer. In addition, women are more likely to be called on to provide long-term care for their spouses, parents, in-laws, or other relatives. The cost of long-term care depends on the arrangement, but it is never inexpensive. Initially, you may want to arrange for in-home care, hiring service providers to take care of tasks that range from cleaning the bathrooms to skilled nursing care.

At some point, your loved one may need more care than you can provide in either their home or your home. When looking for the next level of care, you may consider an assisted living facility, memory care center, or nursing home. Such a move will substantially increase the cost of care. For many individuals, the eventual sale of a home can be used to help cover the cost of long-term care. Medicare pays for long-term care only for specific services such as rehabilitation and only for a very short time period. Medicaid will help pay for long-term care only after an individual's income and assets fall below a certain level.[45] If you are caring for an aging spouse or relative, determine whether they are eligible for any services provided through the Veterans Administration, hospice, or other state, local, or federal health-care programs.

It's never too early to think about your own eventual need for long-term care. Instead of leaving it up to chance and hoping you (or your kids) can figure it out in the moment, consider setting aside an additional amount of your savings to cover the potential costs of long-term care. One option is to set aside the amount you would like to bequeath to your children; that will keep you from jeopardizing the rest of your living expenses. Although you may not end up leaving your heirs as much as you would have liked, at least you won't be burdening them with the expense of your long-term care. You may also want to purchase a long-term care insurance policy, particularly if the need for long-term care runs in your family.

When it comes to long-term care, you essentially have four options: You pay, insurance pays, the government pays, your kids pay. However it plays out, one of these four options or some combination of them will be needed. Decide in advance which you prefer and set about making that a viable option while you still have the chance to choose.

CHAPTER 19

How to Prepare for the Unexpected

WHETHER IT'S AN UNEXPECTED hospitalization, a tree falling on your roof, the loss of a job, or the loss of a spouse, many events have the potential to disrupt your life. Dealing with questions about money during a time of crisis or grief can add to your already high stress levels. That's why one of the best things you can do during calm periods of your life is to make sure your finances are in order and accompanied with detailed instructions should anything happen to you. It's also a good idea to make sure your spouse and your parents or other family members have taken these steps as well. To help you with that process, the following is a short list of items you should have.

A Rainy Day Fund

It's always a good idea to have the equivalent of three to six months of income saved in an easy-to-access account (a savings or checking account; not an IRA or other type of retirement account) to help soften the blow when life doesn't go as planned. Having extra cash is enormously helpful when you unexpectedly need to replace a car or major appliance or if you find yourself suddenly unemployed.

An Updated Résumé

Sometimes you lose your job for reasons far beyond your control. If you find yourself out of work, it will be easier to transition back into the job market if you have been periodically updating your résumé, even while you were happily employed. It's also a good idea to maintain a list of your professional contacts and get in touch with them periodically so that you have a solid professional network you can turn to if you need a new place of employment.

An "Emergency" Money Contact List

I recently had lunch with a group of my mother's friends, several of whom had been widowed. Because they knew my profession, several mentioned how difficult it had been after their husbands passed away to figure out where their money was being held and who was in charge of it. While it's certainly not something anyone wants to think about, the possibility remains that your spouse may pass unexpectedly. I highly encourage everyone, and especially women who are dependent on their spouse's retirement benefits and savings, to make an emergency contact list with your spouse. List all of the accounts you and your spouse own, the primary contact for each account, and the number to call should anything happen.

Revisit the list at least once a year to make sure it stays current. That way, if something does happen, you won't have to fish through old statements or emails during an already difficult time just to maintain your financial solvency. We've included a worksheet in Appendix A to help you get started keeping track of these items.

A Regular Review of Your Will and Wishes

If you don't have a will already, make sure that you and your spouse at least verbally discuss what your final wishes are and who should carry them out. That being said, you need a will. See chapter 11 for more advice on how to draw up a will. It's also a good idea to update your will as major life events occur, particularly when you get married or remarried or when there are additions to the family. You want to be sure your new spouse or grandchild is taken care of in case anything happens to you.

A Good Friend

This may seem like a silly addition to this list, but as I said before, the more stories I hear of unexpected, life-altering events, the more convinced I am that we all need good friends we can turn to without a moment's hesitation. Who would you call right now if you were suddenly facing a death or major illness in your family? If no one comes to mind, you may need to spend some time cultivating relationships (as discussed in chapter 17). Having someone you can lean on who will walk with you through the difficult meetings and take care of logistics for you can be a huge blessing.

While I would not wish tragedy on anyone, life is unpredictable, and you owe it to yourself and your loved ones to consistently make sure your affairs are in order. If you are currently dealing with a difficult situation and would like to speak with someone, you can find my contact info at the back of this book. I am sincerely always happy to listen and help when I can.

PART 6

Being Enough

Decide what your currency is early.
Let go of what you will never have. People who do this are
happier and sexier.

—AMY POEHLER, *YES PLEASE*

If you were to ask me what I believe is the secret sauce to enjoying a successful retirement, I would tell you without a moment's hesitation that it is "having enough." If you were to ask me what I believe is the secret sauce to being confident and living a joy-filled life, I would answer that it is "believing you are enough." As we come to the final section of this book, I hope you've gained greater confidence in your financial literacy and that you've learned some new tips and tricks for saving enough to provide for your financial goals. These last few chapters are a quick word on contentment and why I believe it is so crucial to both your financial successes and to your personal happiness.

CHAPTER 20

Confidence and Contentment

As I previously mentioned, I believe being content is the secret to living a full and happy life. When we choose to live life from a discontented perspective, we make our happiness conditional on achieving the next goal. We are constantly striving, constantly fighting to arrive, constantly telling ourselves lies.

- *Once I'm a size 2, I will be happy.*
- *As soon as I get that promotion, I'll finally be OK.*
- *It will all be right in the world once I'm married and have the designer home in the suburbs with a brand-new minivan and 1.5 children and a perfectly trained golden retriever.*

But the thing is—we never get there. There's always something just out of our reach. As soon as we drop a size we look at ourselves in the mirror and decide that really we need to go down just one more. Once we get the promotion, we immediately consider what title we should pursue next. As long as so and so has a bigger, more beautiful home, ours will never be enough.

Contentment requires us to look around and recognize that what we have *is enough*. Even when it's very little. If you are reading this, then that means you are alive, and that right there should be enough. Every breath is an incredible miracle! Your delicate lungs are filling with oxygen and your heart is pumping that oxygen to your brain and your brain is telling the rest of your body what to do. Your eyes are taking in the symbols on this page and turning them into words that you are comprehending and it's amazing. It's all utterly amazing.

You are enough. Just as you are. No matter what has happened or will happen, you are enough simply because you are you. When you truly let that soak in, wonderful things will happen. Recognizing that you are enough is the foundation for being confident, which is ultimately what this book is all about—being confident with your money and in who you are. Contentment is the key to this confidence.

On the other hand, while you cannot be solely goal-oriented, you also should not spend your whole life sitting at home and letting the world pass you by. It is so vital that you love who you are, but it is also vital that you pursue things and people that give you purpose and remind you of the wonderful ways in which you are uniquely valuable. Never, ever settle for someone or something simply because it's available. One of the worst decisions I ever made was taking a job I didn't like just because it was offered to me when nothing else seemed available. One of the best decisions I have ever made was waiting around for a man who respects me and treats me with kindness and compassion and pushes me to my greatest potential. I was able to wait for him for what felt like forever because I knew my value and wasn't about to waste it on someone who just happened to be there.

I chose to focus on confidence and contentment in the last chapter of this book because I believe they are uniquely intertwined and the secret to living a joy-filled life. The most beautiful people I know are both confident and content. True confidence is stunning, and I am convinced that it stems from being at peace—deep down content—with who you are and what you have.

Genuinely confident, content people are so attractive because they are sure of themselves without being arrogant. When you are genuinely confident in who you are, you do not need to force your confidence on others, which allows you to get to know them and invite them in. Some of my dearest friends have mastered this quality, which is what drew me to them in the first place. They don't demand attention, but they're also not afraid to be who they are. Being content doesn't mean that you have settled for less than you deserve. Being content allows you to put yourself aside and be genuinely interested in others. People who can do this are, in my opinion, the most beautiful people on earth.

Who's in Charge Here?

After my grandmother passed away, I found a sticky note on her laptop. In neat, perfect cursive, she had transcribed the wonderful, yet simple words of the late missionary and pastor Jim Elliot.

He is no fool who gives what he cannot keep to gain what he cannot lose.

That sticky note is now in a plain wooden frame on my desk. It reminds me every day to have perspective.

You see, the thing about money is that it doesn't last. You can't take it with you. It is finite. So you have to decide whether you will be in charge of it or whether it will be in charge of you. I promise, it is always one or the other. You must either learn to be content with what you have or let money and finances rule over you. I believe this to be one of life's many progressive journeys. You never fully arrive, but the older you get, the stronger you become. Slowly but surely, you care less and less about money and more and more about the things that truly matter. Like people.

I hope you have learned more about managing money from this book, but I also hope you have learned that *you* are more important than money. Your value does not lie in how much you have in your bank account. It does not lie in the size of your home or the shine of your car. You are valuable simply because you are you. And the more you realize that who you are and what you have is enough, the happier you will be.

Closing Remarks

We made it! Huzzah! I am so proud of us! I want you to know that I feel so awesome right now because you are reading this. I might be drinking a cup of coffee, doing laundry, eating a cupcake, or changing a diaper, but somewhere my ears are tingling because I know that you, my stranger-friend, are making strides toward financial freedom. I am genuinely so glad that I could share my thoughts with you.

This book has been such a blessing to write because it has allowed me not only to care for others and provide financially minded advice, but also to hear some really neat stories from some really incredible women. For that, I am so thankful.

I hope you feel empowered after reading this book. But even more than that, I hope you know that you are valuable. I hope you choose to surround yourself with people who build you up and graciously remove yourself from the presence of those who bring you down. I hope you choose to value others because when we share what we have, we are often blessed in return. I hope you know that whoever you are, wherever you are, you matter. And as you continue in your journey to financial freedom, I hope you know that I believe in you.

Appendix A
The "Keeping Track of Everything" Worksheet

As I mentioned in chapter 19, you need to keep a list of your accounts along with contact information for each, just in case the unexpected happens.

This excellent exercise can serve as a resource to help familiarize yourself with your finances and serve as a lifeline if there is an emergency in your family. It is crucial that you know what's going on so that life's unexpected events don't catch you entirely off guard. I strongly encourage you to sit down right now and figure out where all your financial accounts are and who to call in an emergency. For the sake of keeping your accounts secure, I would cut out this page and store it somewhere safe alongside other important documents.

We have filled in the first row of the table with an example of a fictional account.

Keeping Track of Everything

TYPE OF ACCOUNT	ACCOUNT	LOCATION	WEBSITE	USERNAME	PASSWORD HINT	CONTACT	PHONE	EMAIL
IRA	$300,000	Schwab	Schwab.com	cake4me	First Dog	June Smith	800.557.8621	June.smith@schwab.com

TYPE OF ACCOUNT	ACCOUNT	LOCATION	WEBSITE	USERNAME	PASSWORD HINT	CONTACT	PHONE	EMAIL

APPENDIX B
Judging Quality

One of the hardest parts of finding professional financial help is knowing who to trust. I work in the financial services industry, and I will admit that I am super wary of everyone else in the industry when it comes to dealing with my own finances. (To this day I do my own taxes despite the fact that it is exhausting and I hate doing it). But, ultimately, if you are not a financial expert, you must trust someone! Finding a trustworthy financial professional can help you avoid expensive mistakes and give you confidence in your long-term plans.

It can help if you know a bit about the various designations that financial advisors can obtain in addition to the requirements for specific "series licenses" that financial professionals should have. The following list gives you an idea of what is required for an individual to offer you financial advice and the designations that I personally believe denote expertise and quality.

Series Licenses (Series 7, 65, and 66)
Governing Body: FINRA
(Financial Industry Regulatory Authority)
Website: brokercheck.finra.org

Each license requires the passing of a multiple-choice exam ranging in length and time depending on the topics covered. Different "series" cover different topics. For example, Series 65 is the *Uniform Investment Adviser Law Exam*, which individuals like myself are required to pass in order to do business as a financial advisor. Series 7 is the *General*

Securities Representative Exam, which is necessary for stockbrokers to trade, and Series 66 is the *Uniform Combined State Law Exam,* which qualifies an individual as both a securities agent and investment advisor representative. There are many other series licenses, but these are the ones you're most likely to come across in the financial planning world.

A candidate must receive a score of 72 percent correct or better to pass. Once a candidate has passed and completed registration, they are entered into FINRA's database, which is searchable by the general public. This allows you, the customer, to search for an advisor using a last name. You can then obtain a detailed report about which licenses they've obtained, where they're registered, and whether or not they have any disciplinary actions against them. FINRA licensing is legally required for an individual to practice in the financial industry, but it has more to do with proving that you know the rules than with proving you are an expert in your given field.

My colleagues and I view the following designations as the top designations in the financial services industry. Each requires a significant amount of studying and testing to obtain, and all are governed by highly respected institutions in the financial industry. You can find a lot more information online about these designations if you want more than my opinion.

CFP® (Certified Financial Planner)
Governing Body: CFP® Board
Website: www.cfp.net

In order to obtain the CFP® designation, a candidate must obtain a bachelor's degree and complete an additional course of study (typically two to three years) at a college or university that offers a financial planning curriculum approved by the CFP® Board of Standards. After the course-work is completed, a candidate will sit for the CFP® exam, a two-day, ten-hour comprehensive test covering tax planning, retirement planning, estate planning, insurance, and investment management.

After passing the exam, a planner must record three years of relevant work experience and agree to comply with the CFP® code of ethics in order to receive the CFP® designation. To keep the CFP® designation, individuals are also required to obtain thirty hours of continuing education every two years and must disclose any disciplinary actions that have been taken against them during the last two years.

CPA (Certified Public Accountant)

Governing Body: Licensed on a state-by-state basis
Website: see state board's website

To become a CPA, a candidate must pass the Uniform Certified Public Accountant Examination. In order to be eligible to sit for the exam, a candidate must have completed 150 hours of college units—the equivalent of five years of schooling or a master's degree in accounting. The sixteen-hour exam is split into four sections covering auditing and attestation, business environment and concepts, financial accounting and reporting, and regulation. Candidates are also required to meet an experience requirement, which varies by state, as well as complete a special exam on the topic of ethics. Like other designations, CPAs must also complete a continuing education requirement on an annual basis.

CFA® (Certified Financial Analyst)

Governing Body: CFA® Institute
Website: www.cfainstitute.org

To obtain the CFA® designation, candidates must have four years of qualified professional investment work experience and have passed all three levels of the CFA® exam. Candidates are expected to spend, on average, around 300 hours studying for each level. The program covers a broad range of topics including ethical and professional standards, fixed-income and equity analysis, economics, financial reporting, alternative and derivative investments, portfolio management, and wealth planning. Each exam lasts six hours. To give you an idea of the level of difficulty, in 2014 the average pass rate across all three exams was 46 percent. Upon obtaining the designation, charterholders must also adhere to the CFA® Institute's Code of Conduct and sign an annual professional conduct statement listing any investigations, litigations, arbitration, complaints, disciplinary actions, and any other matters relating to their professional conduct.

Resources

I am a rule follower, and I like to give credit where credit is due. Here is a list of the sources I borrowed from to create this book.

Angelou, Maya. *Mom & Me & Mom*. New York: Random House, 2013.

Austen, Jane. *Mansfield Park*. Ware: Wordsworth Editions Limited, 1992.

Babcock, Linda, and Sara Laschever. *Women Don't Ask*. New York: Bantam, 2007.

Bank of America. "Deposit Interest Rates & APYs." April 21, 2017. https://media.bac-assets.com/DigitalDeposit_CA.pdf?cacheBuster=218.

Brown, Brené. *Daring Greatly: How the Courage to Be Vulnerable Transforms the Way We Live, Love, Parent, and Lead*. New York: Avery, 2012.

Brown, Brené. *The Gifts of Imperfection: Let Go of Who You Think You're Supposed to Be and Embrace Who You Are*. Center City: Hazelden, 2010.

Buffett, Warren E. "Letter to Shareholders of Berkshire Hathaway Inc." February 28, 2002. http://www.berkshirehathaway.com/2001ar/2001letter.html.

Bugbee, Katie. "How Much Does Child Care Cost?" https://www.care.com/c/stories/2423/how-much-does-child-care-cost/.

Catalyst. "Women In Canadian, US, And Global Financial Services." December 2, 2015. http://www.catalyst.org/knowledge/women-financial-services.

CFA Institute. *CFA Level III Volume 2: Behavioral Finance, Individual Investors, and Institutional Investors*. 2016. CFA Institute, July 2015. VitalBook file.

CFA Institute Research Foundation. "Gender Diversity in Investment Management: New Research for Practitioners on How to Close the Gender Gap." 2016. https://www.cfainstitute.org/learning/future/Documents/gender_diversity_report.pdf.

Coker, Steve. "The Financial Side of Divorce." CedarstoneAdvisors.com, August 5, 2016. https://www.cedarstoneadvisors.com/single-post/2017/09/19/The-Financial-Side-of-Divorce.

College Board. "Trends in College Pricing 2014." 2014. https://secure-media.collegeboard.org/digitalServices/misc/trends/2014-trends-college-pricing-report-final.pdf.

Consumer Federation of America. "Less Than Half of U.S. Households Report Good Savings Progress, According to 2016 America Saves Week Survey." February 22, 2016. http://consumerfed.org/press_release/less-than-half-of-u-s-households-report-good-savings-progress-according-to-annual-america-saves-week-survey/.

Cost of Wedding. "Average Wedding Cost." 2016. http://www.costofwedding.com/.

Credit Sesame. "Guide: Credit Score Range for Experian, Transunion, Equifax." July 26, 2016. https://www.creditsesame.com/blog/credit/credit-score-range-for-experian-transunion-equifax/.

Davis, Elizabeth. "Deductible vs Copayment—What's the Difference?" Verywell, August 16, 2015. http://healthinsurance.about.com/od/faqs/fl/Deductible-vs-Copayment-Whats-the-Difference.htm.

Edwards, Haley Sweetland. "Inside the Next Social Security Crisis." *Time,* July 23, 2015.

Ephron, Nora. "Nora Ephron '62 addressed the graduates in 1996." Wellesley College, 1996.https://www.wellesley.edu/events/commencement/archives/1996commencement.

Fuller, Kate. "Rage in the Safeway Parking Lot." *Grace Sent Me* (blog), December 9, 2015. http://gracesentme.tumblr.com/post/134881821671/rage-in-the-safeway-parking-lot.

Gladwell, Malcolm. "Open Secrets." Gladwell.com, January 8, 2007. http://gladwell.com/open-secrets/.

Health View Services. "2015 Retirement Health Care Costs Data Report." 2015. https://www.hvsfinancial.com/PublicFiles/Data_Release.pdf.

HealthCare.gov. "How Insurance Companies Set Health Premiums." 2017. https://www.healthcare.gov/how-plans-set-your-premiums/.

Hoffman, Allison K., and Howell E. Jackson. "Retiree Out-of-Pocket Healthcare Spending: A Study of Consumer Expectations and Policy Implications." American Journal of Law and Medicine 39, no. 1 (February 10, 2013); UCLA School of Law, Law-Econ Research Paper No. 13–04; Harvard Public Law Working Paper No. 13–14. http://ssrn.com/abstract=2214643.

IRS. "Retirement Topics—IRA Contribution Limits." October 20, 2017. https://www.irs.gov/retirement-plans/plan-participant-employee/retirement-topics-ira-contribution-limits.

IRS. "SEP Plan FAQs—Contributions." 2016. https://www.irs.gov/retirement-plans/retirement-plans-faqs-regarding-seps-contributions.

Kollman, Geoffrey. "Social Security: Summary of Major Changes in the Cash Benefits Program." Social Security website, May 18, 2000. https://www.ssa.gov/history/reports/crsleghist2.html.

Leanse, Ellen Petry. "'Just' Say No." LinkedIn, May 29, 2015. https://www.linkedin.com/pulse/just-say-ellen-petry-leanse.

Lino, Mark. "Expenditures on Children by Families, 2013." August 2014. U.S. Department of Agriculture Center for Nutrition Policy and Promotion.

Marks, Howard. *The Most Important Thing: Uncommon Sense for the Thoughtful Investor.* New York: Columbia Business School Publishing, 2011.

Medicare.gov. "Health Maintenance Organization (HMO) Plan." https://www.medicare.gov/sign-up-change-plans/medicare-health-plans/medicare-advantage-plans/hmo-plans.html.

Medicare.gov. "Preferred Provider Organization (PPO) Plans." https://www.medicare.gov/sign-up-change-plans/medicare-health-plans/medicare-advantage-plans/preferred-provider-organization-plans.html.

Mortgage Calculator. "Introduction to Mortgages: Basic Mortgage Terminology." 2016. https://www.mortgagecalculator.org/helpful-advice/mortgage-terminology.php.

My First Apartment. "Average Utility Bills: My First Apartment Survey Results." July 2015. http://www.myfirstapartment.com/2015/08/average-utility-bill-survey/.

Oliver, Mary. *Upstream: Selected Essays.* New York: Penguin Random House LLC, 2016.

Pfau, W. "Getting on Track for Retirement." Retirement Researcher, June 29, 2011. https://retirementresearcher.com/getting-on-track-for-retirement/.

Poehler, Amy. *Yes Please.* New York: HarperCollins, 2014.

Randolph, Mary. "Probate Shortcuts in California." NOLO. https://www.nolo.com/legal-encyclopedia/california-probate-shortcuts-31777.html.

Randolph, Mary. "Probate Shortcuts in Colorado." NOLO. https://www.nolo.com/legal-encyclopedia/colorado-probate-shortcuts-32195.html.

Sandberg, Sheryl. "Transcript and Video of Speech by Sheryl Sandberg, Chief Operating Officer, Facebook."

Barnard College, May 18, 2011. https://barnard.edu/headlines.
transcript-and-video-speech-sheryl-sandberg-chief-operating-officer-
facebook.

Sandberg, Sheryl. Post on Facebook.com, June 3, 2015. https://www.
facebook.com/sheryl/posts/10155617891025177:0.

Simon-Thomas, Emiliana R. "Are Women More Empathetic Than
Men?" *Greater Good in Action website*, June 1, 2007. http://greatergood.
berkeley.edu/article/item/women_more_empathic_than_men.

Social Security. "Survivors Planner: How Much Would Your Benefit Be?"
Social Security Administration. https://www.ssa.gov/planners/
survivors/ifyou5.html.

State Street Global Advisors and Knowledge@Wharton. "Bridging the
Trust Divide: The Financial Advisor-Client Relationship." *Wharton
University of Pennsylvania*. http://d1c25a6gwz7q5e.cloudfront.net/
papers/download/ssga_advisor_trust_Report.pdf.

Stepp, Erin. "Annual Cost to Own and Operate a Vehicle Falls to $8,698,
Finds AAA." AAA Newsroom, April 28, 2015. http://newsroom.aaa.
com/2015/04/annual-cost-operate-vehicle-falls-8698-finds-aaa/.

The Big Mac Index: Historical Data from the Economist's Big Mac Index.
"Big Mac Index 2015." January 22, 2015. http://bigmacindex.org/.

The Institute for College Access & Success. "Project on Student Debt."
April 27, 2015. https://ticas.org/posd/map-state-data.

USAGov. "Credit Reports and Scores." August 30, 2016. https://www.usa.
gov/credit-reports.

U.S. Department of Health and Human Services. "The Basics."
LongTermCare.gov. https://longtermcare.acl.gov/the-basics/.

United States Department of Agriculture. "Official USDA Food Plans; Cost
of Food at Four Levels." December 2015. http://www.cnpp.usda.gov/
sites/default/files/CostofFoodDec2015.pdf.

United States Department of Labor. "Women in the Labor Force." http://
www.dol.gov/wb/stats/stats_data.htm.

Vanguard. "Learn about Saving for College." Investor Education Series.
2016.

Vanguard. "What's the Average Cost of College?" 2016. https://investor.
vanguard.com/college-savings-plans/average-cost-of-college.

Notes

A complete citation for each endnote can be found under the *Resources* section on page 217.

1 *Catalyst*, "Women in Financial Service" and CFA Institute Research Foundation, "Gender Diversity in Investment Management: New Research for Practitioners on How to Close the Gender Gap."

2 Kate Fuller, "Rage in the Safeway Parking Lot."

3 Brené Brown, *Daring Greatly*.

4 State Street Global Advisors and Knowledge@Wharton, "Bridging the Trust Divide."

5 Emiliana R. Simon-Thomas, "Are Women More Empathetic Than Men?"

6 Warren Buffett, "Letter to Shareholders of Berkshire Hathaway Inc."

7 Bank of America, "Deposit Interest Rates and APYs"

8 The rates have changed over the years, but you can find up-to-date ones on the IRS website.

9 Malcolm Gladwell, "Open Secrets."

10 Definitions taken from CFA Institute, *CFA Level III Volume 2: Behavioral Finance, Individual Investors, and Institutional Investors*.

11 Ibid.

12 Linda Babcock and Sara Laschever, *Women Don't Ask*.

13 *Catalyst*, "Women in Financial Services."

14 CFA Institute Research Foundation, "Gender Diversity in Investment Management: New Research for Practitioners on How to Close the Gender Gap."

15 U.S. Department of Labor, "Women in the Labor Force."

16 Ellen Petry Leanse, "'Just' Say No."

17 Medicare.gov, "Health Maintenance Organization (HMO) Plan."

18 Medicare.gov, "Preferred Provider Organization (PPO) Plans."

19 Elizabeth Davis, "Deductible vs Copayment— What's the Difference?"

20 HealthCare.gov, "How Insurance Companies Set Health Premiums."

21 USA.gov, "Credit Reports and Scores."

22 Credit Sesame, "Guide: Credit Score Range for Experian, TransUnion, Equifax."

23 Ibid.

24 Ibid.

25 The Institute for College Access & Success, "Project on Student Debt."

26 As of fall of 2017.

27 Cost of Wedding, "Average Wedding Cost."

28 IRS, "SEP Plan FAQs—Contributions."

29 College Board, "Trends in College Pricing 2014."

30 Vanguard, "What's the Average Cost of College?"

31 Vanguard, "Learn about Saving for College."

32 Care.com, "How Much Does Child Care Cost?"

33 NOLO, "Probate Shortcuts in Your State."

34 Mortgage Calculator, "Introduction to Mortgages."

35 Consumer Federation of America, "Less Than Half of U.S. Households Report Good Savings Progress."

36 BigMacIndex.

37 Haley Sweetland Edwards, "Inside the Next Social Security Crisis."

38 Geoffrey Kollman, "Social Security: Summary of Major Changes in the Cash Benefits Program."

39 Social Security, "Survivors Planner: How Much Would Your Benefit Be?"

40 Allison K. Hoffman and Howell E. Jackson, "Retiree Out-of-Pocket Healthcare Spending."

41 HealthView Services, "2015 Retirement Health Care Costs Data Report."

42 Steve Coker, "The Financial Side of Divorce."

43 Sheryl Sandberg, Facebook.com.

44 U.S. Department of Health and Human Services, "The Basics."

45 Ibid.

Acknowledgements

With any large project, there are a lot of people to thank. In an ideal world, I would put all of their names on the cover, but no one lets me do what I want.

First of all, I'd like to thank my company, which, contrary to my previous statement, often lets me do what I want, including write this book. Specifically, I'd like to extend a great deal of gratitude to both Matt Davis and Steve Coker for checking all of my financial wisdom for financial accuracy. If you didn't like the book, it's probably their fault in some way (just kidding, they're the best!).

I'd also like to thank my editing and creative team for being incredibly good at what they do. Extra thanks to Cecily Breeding, who continually makes my creative dreams come true and who is pretty much a real-life superwoman. And to my editor, Tammy Ditmore, who is the smartest person I have ever worked with and should be given all of the credit if you liked this book. You are both amazing. Thank you. Thank you. Thank you.

To my husband, who puts up with way more of my shenanigans than he should, thereby proving once and for all that he is in fact a real-life alien robot—I love you from here to the moon and back.

Finally, I'd like to acknowledge the women that have taught me what it means to be enough. To my incredible friends: Grace, Kelsey, Cassie, Kendra, Marylyn, June, Krista, Callie, Allegra, Kira, Dana, and so many more—thank you for teaching me joy, love, hospitality, authenticity, and for consistently showing me grace. My life is full because of your friendship. To my Nanny, who first read me the poem *Phenomenal Woman* by the great Maya Angelou—thank you for showing me commitment, perseverance, and what it means to be phenomenal. You have diligently cared for many and been rarely acknowledged, but your efforts have not gone unnoticed—at least not by me.

To my mother, who raised me and helped mold my character—thank you for sacrificing your comfort and preferences so that I would know what it means to be loved unconditionally. To my precious baby girl—growing and raising you has been a lot of work but the most worthwhile journey I have ever traveled. I hope you come to know that you are always enough and that I will always love you.

And finally, to my Fritzie, who quietly and yet deeply cared for the people around her on earth while she longed for heaven. I can only hope to be half of the stubborn, grace-filled woman that you were. I love you and I miss you. Thank you for seeing the value in me.

About the Author

 Hannah Boundy is a wife, momma, friend, and financial analyst at Cedarstone Advisors in Westlake Village, California (www.cedarstoneadvisors.com). She is an avid consumer of cupcakes and, consequently, a begrudging runner. Her research centers around the intersection between seeking out financial value and caring for people, which includes research on behavioral biases, fundamental investing, stewardship, and contentment. She loves books, beautiful pianos, and fireplaces. She was lucky enough to marry her sworn enemy who has since become her best friend. She currently resides in Denver, Colorado. You can find more of her financial musings at www.cedarstonecupcakeclub.com. If you'd like to chat about cake or money stuff, you can contact her at hannah.boundy@cedarstoneadvisors.com or reach her at 888.571.5582.

Index